LOVE THAT WORKS

Love that Works

How the Ancient Hebrew Concept of Chesed (hĕ´- sĕd) Creates Marriages, Families and Communities of Covenantal Love that Endure

by Blair Adams

© Copyright 1992, 1997, 1999, 2011 Colloquium Press Trust

Excerpted from *Leaving the Lonely Labyrinth: Seeking Enduring Love as the Only Rule of Life in an Age of Narcissism and Manipulation, Betrayal and Cynicism, Violence and Ephemeral Connections* by Blair Adams, copyright 1977, 1988, 1999, 2007 Colloquium Press Trust.

All rights reserved. No part of this publication may be reproduced, stored in a retrieval system, or transmitted in any form by any means, electronic, mechanical, photocopy, recording or otherwise, without the prior permission of the publisher, except as provided by USA copyright law.
080715/UD-1118F

Published by

Colloquium Press
www.colloquiumpress.com

Printed in the United States of America

Dedication

To Denny Allensworth, who knew what it meant to keep *chesed*.

Contents

Love that Works
How the Ancient Hebrew Concept of Chesed (hĕ´- sĕd) Creates Marriages, Families and Communities of Covenantal Love that Endure 1
   Chesed 7
      The Surrender of Our Own Identity 14
      The Poetry and Prose of Committed Love 18
      The Pillar and Ground of a Transcendent Order 21
      The Specificity of True Commitment 35
      The Mercy of Chesed 43
      The Courage to Be Vulnerable 53
   Our Debt of Love 65
   An Active Love 72
   Chesed and Words to Stand By 83
   Fulfillment versus Satisfaction 92
   Infinite Passion 95
   The Pseudo-Love of Seduction 101
   Form and Fulfillment 104
   Precision and Sincerity 110

Notes 137

LOVE THAT WORKS

How the Ancient Hebrew Concept of Chesed (hĕ´- sĕd) Creates Marriages, Families and Communities of Covenantal Love that Endure

∽

"It is not your love that sustains marriage, but from now on, the marriage that sustains your love."

DIETRICH BONHOEFFER

Many Christians believe that each person faces the major decision of his or her life in choosing whether to accept or reject God's offer to enter into life's ultimate covenant, the New Covenant relationship with the Lord Jesus Christ. But even among professed Christians, many also try to evade the implications this decision has for the remainder of their lives. They do so by finding a lesser but counterfeit covenant with Christ that frees them from all responsibility, submission or obedience to God. Or else they truncate the covenant into something of major concern *only* in the initial *making* of it. But to them, actually living out one's life in the covenant remains of peripheral concern. Ingenious doctrines have been invented to cover all these purposes of pushing to the periphery the daily living of one's life in a real and viable relationship of obedience to God.

But we shall see that the New Covenant involves, in fact, a decision to enter into a covenant that assumes a form very much like that initiated by traditional marriage vows, at least in that long lost time ago when they were still considered irrevocable and inviolable. As such a vow, the New Covenant is, of course, distinguished as the covenant that carries a sense of ultimacy in terms of solemnity and sacredness. It therefore far exceeds in weightiness even the traditional marriage vows. If a covenant is a "relationship under sanctions," as Meredith Kline has defined it, then the greatest covenant and the greatest sanctions must surely come with entering a direct relationship with God.[1] This is what constitutes the marriage between the Bridegroom, Christ, and His Bride, the church.*
This is the means by which people make the weighty

---

* Matt. 25:1-13; John 3:28-29; Eph. 5:22-32; Rev. 22:17.

decision for inclusion in His kingdom, a decision that comes when they join themselves together with Him in the exclusive covenant He Himself has initiated. Biblically, this decision has not come until they accept the commitment of submission to Him in the same way that a Biblical bride would have acknowledged her commitment to her husband, by taking on his name.*

As shown in another study,† *Yahweh* is God's covenantal name. This is the name through which He manifests Himself in covenant relationship to His people. And *Yah*shua—Jesus—is the fulfilled revelation to humankind of that covenantal name of *Yah*weh. Just as a traditional bride takes on her husband's name, so the Bride of Christ must be joined, through a covenant pledge, to her heavenly Husband, and this is done in His covenantal name.‡ Each constituent member of that Bride will have at some point walked escorted on the arm of the heavenly Father (the eternal Spirit of Yahweh that has drawn them to

---

* See Gen. 2:19-20, 23; 3:16; Num. 6:27; Ps. 61:5; Isa. 4:1; 26:13, NIV; 63:19; 1 Kings 14:21; 2 Kings 21:4, 7; 2 Chron. 7:14; Jer. 15:16; Amos 9:12; Eph. 3:15; 1 Cor. 11:3, 7-9; 1 Tim. 2:9-14; Titus 2:4-5; 1 Pet. 3:1-6; Acts 2:38; 8:16; 10:48; 19:5.

† See *Knowing God by Name* by Blair Adams (Elm Mott, Tex.: Colloquium Press, 1977, 1988, 2010).

‡ See *Belonging to God* (1977, 1988, 2014) and *Troubled Waters* (1977, 1999, 2010) both by Blair Adams (Elm Mott, Tex.: Colloquium Press).

the person of Christ) and to the altar of Calvary where a battered and scarred Bridegroom waits to receive them unto Himself, not only into His divine and resurrected life but also into the abused and suffering identity of His sacrificial death when He came to earth as a man.* Once at the altar, believers agree to pour themselves into the form that the temple, which is His church, presents to us (Eph. 1:22-23; 2:19-22; Col. 1:17-19, 24). In other words, we pour out our souls on the temple's altar of repentance, in death to our old identity. This outpouring does not stop until our lives commingle with Christ's in His sacrifice and suffering, until we are completely one with Him in His death, His burial and His resurrected life (Rom. 6:3-5; 8:11-17). This unfolding course *is* the gospel (1 Cor. 15:1-4). And it is obedience to this gospel that makes us know we have abandoned our old fallen identity by dying to it and burying it into Christ's righteousness, by burying it into a life conformed to His own sacrifice.†

It is only then, in full consciousness of what we are doing, that we can truly say, "I will," to the question of whether we, "forsaking all others," will unite ourselves to this God and to His Body, His people. And this we will do "for better or for worse, in sickness

---

* Isa. 52:14; 53:2-10; Luke 9:23; Gal. 2:20; 1 Pet. 2:20-24; 1 John 2:6.

† Rom. 6:3-7; 8:29; 1 Pet. 2:19-24; 1 John 3:16; Phil. 2:5-8.

and in health, for richer, for poorer, from this time forth even forevermore." Our surrender unto Him is an *enduring* submission, a faithfulness "even unto death" (Rev. 12:11, ESV). The relationship also calls for us to be filled with the resurrection Spirit that sows God's very nature within us.* We must then walk on in that Spirit until the seed comes to fruition, until we reach maturity in God's plenary image, "the full grain in the head" (Mark 4:28)—only then can the harvesting of our lives come to pass as a harvest unto eternal life.

To enter this marriage vow of exclusive commitment is, in the Hebrew of the Old Testament, to enter into the *b'rit*. *B'rit* is the Hebrew word for "covenant." It constituted the celebration, "the ceremony of innocence," the act of a pure conscience and conviction by which the initiate came into an enduring relationship. And whether with God or man, it was always a relationship accompanied by sanctions.[2] It was the pledge of entrance into the covenant, even into the covenantal nation initiated by God. So, among the Jews, the circumcision was known as the *b'rit*. In the New Covenant, spiritual circumcision is associated with water baptism—that is, with what the Jews saw as the *mikveh* (Rom. 2:28-29; Col. 2:11-13). When someone makes the *b'rit*, he binds himself to those

---

* Acts 2:1-4, 38; Eph. 1:13; 1 Pet. 1:23; 1 John 3:9.

with whom he enters into covenant. To make the *b'rit* with God acknowledges the nature of the covenant commitment that He asks of us to make. It states that we desire to enter into that covenant in full view of all its terms, conditions and sanctions, and we do so in the presence of witnesses. It means we recognize, first, the commitments made, next, the exclusiveness of covenants (such as marriage, including the marriage of the Lamb), then, the total nature of this commitment, and, finally, that, by entering into the *b'rit*, we declare our unshakable conviction that we will remain faithful to the covenant all the days of our lives.

Perhaps most important to the seriousness of the covenant is that we are confessing our recognition of the sanctions that stand against us if we betray it (Heb. 10:29). Through this covenant, we have entered into Christ's death (Rom. 6:3-7). So to betray it is to have the curse, which this death was to remove, fall upon us with explicit force (Gal. 3:13). Therefore, we, in fact, declare our recognition of all that the covenant entails, as well as our determination to remain absolutely and unfailingly faithful to it.

CHESED

To make a *pledge* of faithfulness to the covenant and all of its conditions only *begins* the journey of faith. And people who say things like, "The journey is everything, the destination is nothing" or, "The journey *is* the destination" are not going to understand this sort of journey. It is not an air bubble journey that can be described by trendy and trite slogans. It is not, in short, for those who have never had to deal with life's tough realities. People who know that every time they fall they won't land on a feather bed won't place much confidence in Pollyanna slogans or prophecies. They know that real-life journeys can become as dismaying and crushing as a journey through a waterless wasteland. And if there's no destination where water can be found, they're not going to be mouthing empty platitudes about the journey being everything. So there will be times when, after we've pledged faithfulness to a covenant, it will take all the courage we have, and then some we don't yet have, to keep placing one foot in front of another, and keep walking faithfully in what we have pledged.

Just as the wedding ceremony marks only the beginning of the actual marriage relationship, so our pledge of covenantal faithfulness to God marks only the beginning of our marriage to Him within the community of *His* design. The Hebrews had a special term to denote this *continuing* faithfulness to the covenant. This special term distinguished it from the initial vow to faithfulness and fidelity. The term was *chesed.**

The Biblical story of Ruth depicts the Hebrew meaning of this term. This is somewhat ironic in that Ruth was not a Hebrew but a Gentile Moabitess.[†] Ruth had married into the Jewish family of Naomi. Years before, Naomi's family had journeyed to the land of Moab because of famine in their native Bethlehem, a place name that means, "House of Bread." So another irony was that *famine* had struck the "House of Bread." In any case, when the famine had long since ended and her sons had died, Naomi bid her daughters-in-law good-bye. She even discouraged them from returning to Israel with her. The two sons of Naomi whom they had married had died in Moab, and Naomi had no more sons.

Also, as an Israelite of a noted family, Naomi could hardly have been ignorant of God's command in the twenty-third chapter of Deuteronomy: "No . . . Moabite or any of his descendants may enter

---

* The initial *ch* is pronounced as in the words *loch* or *Bach*. The stress is on the first syllable.

[†] See *Leaving the Lonely Labyrinth* by Blair Adams (Elm Mott, Tex.: Colloquium Press, 1977, 1988, 2007).

the assembly of Yahweh . . . . Do not seek a treaty of friendship with them *as long as you live* . . . . You shall *not* seek their peace or their prosperity all your days *forever*" (Deut. 23:3, 6, NIV, NASB, Ampl.). We would not be surprised to discover that this, at least partly, was what constrained Orpah to stay behind and what compelled Naomi to urge her to do so.

Though Orpah apparently had intended to return with Naomi, when Naomi made clear she had nothing more to offer her daughters-in-law and that they should therefore return to their own people and their own gods among the Gentiles, Orpah wept, but only because her kiss was one of good-bye. But while Orpah was walking away from Naomi, "Ruth clung to her" mother-in-law. Naomi then entreated Ruth also: "'Behold, your sister-in-law is going back to her people, and to her gods; return after your sister-in-law."

Yet, although Ruth was a Moabitess, from a people "forever" severed from the covenant of Israel (Deut. 23:3-6; Neh. 13:1-2), she had the faith of Abraham, the faith to leave her country and kinsmen and wander as a stranger to a land where she knew the people would likely despise those of her origins (Gen. 12:1-5; Deut. 23:3-6). In spite of this, she uttered her fateful words of covenant commitment to her mother-in-law, Naomi: "Entreat me not to leave you, or to return from following after you; for where you go, I will go; and where you lodge, I will lodge: your people shall be my people, and your God, my God. Where you die, I will die, and there I will be buried: Yahweh do so to me, and more also, if anything but death parts you and me" (Ruth 1:15-17, KJV, NIV). This was essentially a pledge of death to her old identity in hopes that she might find a new identity in the people of God.

Ruth knew that this covenant vow would place her in a new and foreign homeland, in the service of a poor widow without any sons to care for the woman's needs, and with no prospect of anything that might personally benefit herself. This situation makes even more startling Ruth's contrast to her Moabite sister Orpah, not only in her willingness to speak those fateful words for entering into the *b'rit* (covenant) of Israel but, even more, also in her unfolding faithfulness to that *b'rit*. She made the vow, she entered the covenant with sanctions, but then, most importantly, she remained loyal and faithful to it.

As part of Ruth's *chesed* to Naomi, she went into the barley fields to gather the gleanings for the poor, following behind the lowest of the field hands, happily humbling herself in order to provide for Naomi's needs. Then later, when Naomi instructed her to go and offer herself as a wife to an older man, Boaz, in fulfillment of her covenant obligation to carry on the name and line of her dead husband (Naomi's son), she willingly complied, with no thought for herself. So it happened that Boaz, the kinsman-redeemer, praised Ruth as a woman of *chesed* because of her faithfulness to her commitment to care for her mother-in-law, Naomi: "Yahweh bless you, my daughter . . . . This *chesed* is greater than that which you showed earlier" (Ruth 3:10).

So Ruth obeyed Naomi's instruction to look to the older Boaz as her kinsman-redeemer, the one who would become her husband. And this obedience became her second act of *chesed*. She did this rather than look to the younger men of Israel as potential husbands. When she later married Boaz, Ruth also fulfilled her covenant obligation as the widow of the deceased Mahlon—in other words, she continued his name in Israel through marriage within his bloodline (Ruth 4:5, 10), for Boaz was his near kinsman. When Ruth fulfilled this duty of the Mosaic Law, she showed the measure of her covenant commitment, her love, to God and to Naomi and to Naomi's family—in short, to the entire order of transcendence that constituted the community of Israel. To say it another way, she showed in deed that she was no longer a Moabitess but an Israelite. To Ruth, the honor of this community and its God loomed far above and beyond her own personal concerns and desires.

Moreover, Boaz also proved himself a man of *chesed*, for he gladly received as his bride this woman from the cursed Moabite nation. Although a man of wealth and prominence, he praised Ruth for seeking him as a husband and entered into the marriage covenant with joy, even though he knew that the children of their union would carry on the name of his dead kinsman rather than his own. From this unselfish Jewish man and this unselfish Gentile woman, both of whom sought to be faithful to their community covenantal obligations, and who did so far beyond seeking their own interests or desires, instead seeking to uphold *chesed*, sprang the Davidic line, the line that would give birth to the Messiah of both Jews and Gentiles, making of the two people one, in one of the world's great reconciliations of love.

When Ruth asks Boaz to spread his "wing [*kanaf*]" over her (Ruth 3:9), the use here of the word "wing" refers to his cloak, which he places over her to express the covering he will provide for her among his people and as her husband. Yet her request here also echoes the blessing that Boaz had pronounced on Ruth when he first encountered her gleaning in his grain field. There, he told her that he knew how she had left her natural family and the country of her birth to serve her Israelite mother-in-law, and then he had said: "The Lord recompense your work and a full reward be given you by the Lord God of Israel *under whose wings you have come for refuge*" (Ruth 2:11-12, NKJV, KJV). (Scholars note that "the word for *robe* in Hebrew is the same as the word for *wing*,"[3] the

Hebrew word *kanaf*. And this image of the *kanaf*, the "wings" of God, also finds expression in the design of the temple in Jerusalem where God was said to reside above the mercy seat of the Ark of the Covenant in the Holy of Holies, a place flanked and covered by winged cherubim. The Psalms frequently present this image of seeking "refuge in the shadow of [God's] wings": Ps. 17:8; 36:7; 57:1; 61:3-4; 63:7; 91:1-4, 9. That is, it meant to marry God.)

So when Boaz spread the corner of his cloak, his *kanaf*, over Ruth, he was declaring that he would join himself in marriage to this woman, who had come seeking refuge under God's wings, under God's *kanaf*, God's order for arranging and covering human relationships. But his pledge to do this ramified in meanings that went far beyond being joined conjugally to this woman. It was the pledge of his selfless willingness to surrender his very identity to continue the name and family lineage of another, the lineage of Naomi's deceased husband and of his son, the man who had been Ruth's husband. And so Boaz's pledge was not only to Ruth but to Naomi, to Naomi's people and to Naomi's God, and ultimately it was the fulfillment of the purpose of that God—for through this marriage would come forth Israel's king, David, and the Son of David who would bring deliverance to all of God's people.

This merger of the meanings of conjugal marriage

and marriage to God and to His people is made explicit in Ezekiel. There, God Himself spreads the corner of His garment, His *kanaf*, over His covenant bride: "'When I passed by you again and looked upon you, indeed your time was the time of love; so *I spread My wing* [alt. *the corner of My garment*] over you and covered your nakedness. Yes, *I swore an oath* to you and *entered into a covenant* with you, and you became Mine,' says the Lord GOD. 'Then I *washed you in water*; yes, I thoroughly washed off your blood, and I *anointed you with oil*'" (Ezek. 16:8-9). So, again, to come under God's wing is to become His covenant bride by submitting and entering the covering provided in His temple, which is His Body.*

The Surrender of Our Own Identity

It is through Boaz's faithfulness to the covenant with God, as well as his complete surrender of himself to God, that Boaz established and carried on the purpose and order of God. It is altogether fitting, therefore, that his name should be the same as one of the two pillars standing beside the entrance of the great temple of Jerusalem: *Yachin* and *Boaz*. Scholars tell us that these "names have a significant symbolic function"—they are what these "biblical

---

*John 2:19-21; Eph. 1:22-23; Col. 1:18, 24; 1 Cor. 10:16-17; 11:1-3, 23-29; 1 Pet. 2:5.

scholars call sentence names." Together they mean: "By his strength (*be-ozzo*, following the Greek) God has established (*yachin*) the world."[4]

These "temple pillars had a two-fold function in the ancient Near East: They not only held up the lintel over the doorway; they also held the firmament in place over the entire earth."[5] Boaz's name is, then, an allusion to the pillar of the temple, and his *chesed*, his covenant faithfulness, is the kind of faithfulness to "establish" God's purpose on earth that upholds God's entire covenantal order. That "strength" in faithfulness to "establish" God's purpose on earth marks the point of entrance into the temple, the place through which we come into the sublime order of the temple, under the "wings" of Yahweh, and begin to take our place in fulfilling the church's corporate function as the "pillar and ground of the truth" (1 Tim. 3:15). Through this process we become those "lively stones" (1 Pet. 2:5, KJV) situated in that "building" that is being "fitly framed together" to grow into a "holy temple in the Lord" (Eph. 2:21, KJV), until each of us, too, can become an overcomer who serves as "a pillar in the temple of . . . God" (Rev. 3:12). A people who struggle to bring their lives and relationships into harmony with God's design thereby help uphold the order, not just of *human* relationships, but of the very cosmos that had been originally ordered by God and then placed under human dominion (Gen. 1:26-30).

To refuse to conform to and bear the responsibility of standing in our place in this order is to invite the continuing collapse of the cosmic order until it becomes complete and nothing remains that can be redeemed or restored.

In the beginning, man and woman failed in the purpose of establishing God's eternal order in creation. Instead, they became instruments through which death entered, leading to ultimate cosmic destruction. But God pledged from the time of the Fall that He would redeem His creation (Gen. 3:15; Rom. 8:19-22). His whole unfolding work with the nation of Israel was in preparation for the fulfillment of this promise. When He brought the Israelites out of Egypt, God had commanded them that they should "seek the place where Yahweh your God chooses . . . to put His name for His dwelling place; and *there you shall go*" (Deut. 12:5). This referred to the temple, for God said to Solomon concerning the temple in Jerusalem: "I have consecrated this house which you have built to put My name there forever, and My eyes and My heart will be there perpetually" (1 Kings 9:3). God also commanded His people that they should not worship Him in the "way" of the nations (Deut. 12:1-4, 8, 11-14, 29-32). God was intent on revealing Himself to them on His own terms, not theirs, and would continue to do so. From the beginning of the entire unfolding relationship, God had established the primacy of His own identity as expressed in a Being of redemptive and incorruptible love. So He, not fallen humanity, would also therefore define and order this sacred love. Although no one would be forced to approach Him, if they did choose to do so, it could never succeed if they did so according to the way of their own choosing or at the place of their own choosing (Deut. 12:5, 13). God, the Giver of life, now Himself designated and prescribed a definite but living form or pattern for life. This alone was how they might legitimately (that is, covenantally) approach Him and come into saving relationship with Him. Through a people who would walk in the path marked out by those like Boaz and Ruth, He would redeem all those who would willingly come under His wings and enter the temple of His new creation, the temple He Himself would establish through His incarnated life of perfect obedience unto death on the cross.

And the entrance to that new cosmic order would be the place at which we surrender our identity completely. Just as Boaz and Ruth did in their upholding of their covenant obligations to each other, to God's people and ultimately to God Himself, here is where we devote our entire existence to carrying on the lineage of Him who bears the name above every name, the Son of David, the son of Jesse, the son of Obed, the son of Boaz and Ruth.

The Poetry and Prose of Committed Love

Chesed, then, becomes the content of the *b'rit* that shows it to be real and not a sham. *Chesed* shows that love is more than a few rare and dazzling flights of poetry—it is also the daily walk of prose. It is more than a dramatic, punctiliar act of faith—it is a *life* of fidelity, obedience and faithfulness. Yet the story of Ruth further teaches that there is art and beauty to both the *b'rit* and *chesed*. Moreover, in the end the prose will better show love's strength, endurance and power to prevail in the details, intricacies and complexities of real life relationships. The story of Ruth shows, in short, that "love never fails." So the poetry of love may reside in its moving profession, as in Ruth's words of covenant commitment to Naomi. But the prose lives out the profession, as in Ruth's gleaning from the fields, in her support of her mother-in-law and then in her marriage to Boaz. The poetry of love inspires us to value and then to make the covenant, the *b'rit*. But then the prose of love takes over in the lovingkindness, the care, the mercy, the fidelity, the determination and all the hard work that applies the *b'rit* to the duties of daily life.

The vows, then, into which we enter when we make our covenant go beyond vague and general principles of faithfulness to commitments, to exclusive loyalties, to a sacred separation (or sacralization) of our lives in the community that *is* the corporate Christ (1 Cor. 12:4-14). Rather, our vows and oaths involve concrete and *specific* commitments, an exclusive relationship with *definite* people, a sacred separation unto a *particular* culture and community, one whose cause and interests will transcend all our own because the community itself expresses the order and life on earth of the transcendent God. For people today, that community is, of course, the spiritual Body of Christ. We enter into that Body, choosing our Kinsman-Redeemer, Christ, as Ruth chose Boaz. We choose Him above all the passing relationships, material possessions, latest fashions and stylish trends of any age—all the "young men" Ruth could have sought (Heb. 11:25-26).

Yet we cannot enter into direct commitments with every member of the global Body of Christ equally and simultaneously. We each stand circumscribed by the limits of our finite creaturehood—we are not God, and, whatever else it may be, it is surely not faith to act as if we were. Technology may offer us the illusion of real relationships that supposedly extend to the ends of the earth, but it doesn't take much reflection to realize that this is all it is—an *illusion*. We each must inevitably fall far short of the infinite reach that only God possesses. He alone can join Himself in a direct and meaningful relationship with every member of the Body of Christ. So while we must love and appreciate all our brothers and sisters in Messiah, even those who remain personally unknown to us, we clearly cannot join ourselves in direct relationship with them all. As said, to think of ourselves as being equally committed in this way to everyone, at least so far as *direct relationship* and loving care goes, in reality means to commit to *no one* but ourselves and our own inflated image, interests and ambitions. It means that, though *in theory* we belong to everyone, we *in fact* belong to no one.

In practical terms, it says that, in spite of all our poetic declarations, no one can in fact depend upon us, that we are totally independent and self-determined, cut off from the flexible but "fixed order" of God's rule of love and from all the relationships built on it. It means that we live all but solely for ourselves and either give our lives to no one or else mete out our lives in teaspoon measures agreeable to our selfishness. Such a view of what it means to be a Christian could not, then, stand more starkly opposed to true *chesed* as manifest in the self-sacrificing love of Christ.

Yet if, as the apostle John declared, we do not love God whom we cannot see unless we love our brothers "whom we can see" (1 John 4:20), then with at least equal certainty we cannot love our brothers whom we cannot see unless we love those brothers whom we *can* see. Within the universal Body of Christ, God has therefore joined us to His Body through concrete, specific relationships, *covenant* relationships that connect us to particular members of a particular local body—*specific* and concrete individuals, ministries and fellowships. *Chesed* will always unfold in the context of those specific fellow Christians "we *can* see."

The Pillar and Ground of a Transcendent Order

Obviously, when we marry, we join ourselves to a specific husband or a specific wife. Yet this is not our only specific commitment in the fixed order of heaven upheld by the pillars of the temple. As redeemed believers submit to the order of love that God is establishing within His Body, the church, as said, stands as "the *pillar* and ground of the truth" (1 Tim. 3:15). Those who remain faithful to the living order of God—to the relationships God has ordained within His covenant Body—are said, in Biblical terminology, to keep *chesed*. But this keeping of *chesed*, of covenant faithfulness, is then portrayed as accomplishing something truly amazing: the Bible describes it as maintaining God's dominion over the order of creation. Thus Paul first writes: "He put *all things* under His feet, and *gave Him to be head over all things to the church, which is His body,* the fullness of Him who fills all in all" (Eph. 1:22-23). This is a quote from Psalms where all "the works of [God's] hands"—that is, all creation—are described and enumerated as standing somehow under human dominion (Ps. 8:3-8). And later in Colossians Paul further writes: "*He is the head of the body, the church*, who is the beginning, the firstborn from the dead, *that in all things He may have the preeminence*" (Col. 1:18). So, in keeping with Ephesians and Psalm 8:6, Paul ties Christ's Headship over His Body, over the church, to His preeminence over the entire universe—"*all* things," including the firmament.

Therefore those who truly keep *chesed* will never treat as something casual or peripheral the order of relationships God has established for His kingdom, the order through which He not only reigns as Head of His Body but by which He also upholds the firmament of the heavens. This is the order of relationships through which we all behold each other with unveiled faces (2 Cor. 3:18) and reflect the light of Jesus Christ (the "sun of righteousness") through the fixed order of the church and the people of God (the "moon" and the "stars").* Only as we're composed and arranged into this great order of God can we

---

*See Gen. 37:9-11; Ps. 19:4-5; 84:11; 89:34-37; 136:7-9; Isa. 60:18-20; Ezek. 32:7-8; Dan. 12:1-3; Joel 2:10, 31; 3:15; Mal. 4:2; Matt. 13:43; 17:2; 24:29; Luke 21:25; Rev. 1:16; 10:1; 12:1; 2 Cor. 3:17-18; Phil. 2:15, NIV.

reflect the Lord into the lives of our brothers and sisters by the light of His Word, and thus contribute to establishing Christ's preeminence over all things in heaven and on earth, upholding the very firmament.

But in Matthew 24, Jesus speaks of the coming time of apostasy, which will be a period of social chaos and continual warfare, a Hobbesian state of nature, when "the *sun* will be darkened" and "the *moon* [turned] into blood" (Joel 2:31; Acts 2:20), when persecutors will "deliver you up to tribulation and kill you, and you shall be hated by all nations for My name's sake. And then many will be offended, will betray one another, and will hate one another. Then many false prophets will rise up and deceive many. And because lawlessness will abound, the love of most will wax cold" (Matt. 24:6-12, NKJV, KJV, NIV). In short, what holds people together in God's order of relationships—love—will cease to function. And so to this account Mark adds: "Now brother will betray brother to death, and a father his child; and children will rise up against parents and cause them to be put to death" (Mark 13:12). This is the breakdown of *chesed* in the entire familial order of Christ's Body. And these events are all connected to a time when "the *sun* will be darkened, and the *moon* will not give its light; the *stars* will fall from heaven, and the *powers of the heavens* [or the firmament] will be shaken" (Matt. 24:29), a time when the fixed order of the heavens will collapse. So the breakdown of God's fixed order of the heavens is explicitly tied to an apostatizing from His fixed order of human and family relationships under God's fatherhood—an order of relationships that, as shown extensively elsewhere,* can only be effectively maintained, particularly in this apostatizing age, within the church. Here the pillars of *the temple*, Boaz and Yachin, fall in unfaithfulness, and so the very order of the firmament falls with them.

The book of Hebrews places the church's devotion to God's order as pivotal in determining that which can be shaken and that which remains unshakable. Hebrews quotes Haggai's Old Testament prophecy, "Yet once more I will shake not only the earth but also heaven" (Heb. 12:26; Hag. 2:6; Joel 3:16). The scripture then warns, "Now this, 'Yet once more,' indicates the removal of those things that are being shaken, as of things that are made, that the things which cannot be shaken may remain" (Heb. 12:27). These scriptures foretell a time when the order of the fallen cosmos will be shaken to its core, first, on earth with the collapse of the pillars of an apostate church and the apostate culture built upon it, and then in

---

* See *What Kind of Family? Innovative Myths, Traditional Religion and the Art of Human Relationships* (1976, 1994, 2011), *Saving Marriage, Family and Community* (2007, 2010) and *Forming Christ's Body, Books One, Two* and *Three* (1977, 1992, 2011), all by Blair Adams (Elm Mott, Tex.: Colloquium Press).

the firmament above, leaving only that which is of a radically different, unshakable order.

So the context for these scriptures is the announcement that believers "have come to *Mount Zion* and to *the city* of the living God, the *heavenly Jerusalem*, . . . to the general assembly and church of the firstborn who are enrolled in heaven" (Heb. 12:22-23, NASB). But these scriptures warn those coming to the "church of the firstborn" that they must "not refuse Him who is speaking. For if those ["those" of the Old Covenant that merely represented through types and shadows the reality of the New (Heb. 8:1-6)] did not escape when they refused Him who warned them on earth, much *less* will we escape who turn away from Him who warns from heaven" (Heb. 12:25, ESV, NKJV). The church whose Head still speaks from heaven must stand against the spirit of apostasy, a spirit that sweeps away the harlot church in the flood of worldly corruption and carries Babylon to her fall. This apostate spirit "turns [people] away from Him who warns from heaven." For only those who hearken and obey, Hebrews concludes, will "receive a *kingdom* that *cannot be shaken*" and should therefore "serve God acceptably with reverence and godly fear" (Heb. 12:28). That which "cannot be shaken" appears on earth as believers listen to and obey the voice of the Spirit as it orders a kingdom on earth just "as it is in heaven" (Matt. 6:10).

The writer of Hebrews precedes his discourse concerning what can and cannot be shaken by explaining the necessary place of discipline in a believer's life (Heb. 12:3-17). For the New Testament tells us that apart from such discipline, no one can claim to be a son within the familial order of God's kingdom (Heb. 12:8). Again, only that which is ordered by God will remain within the kingdom that cannot be shaken, a part of that New Testament temple built upon the immovable Rock.

Just as Paul calls the corporate church "the pillar and ground of the truth," so Jesus tells individuals who "have kept My Word and have not denied My name" and who have "kept the word of My perseverance" that He will "keep [them] from the hour of testing" that will shake the heavens and earth and that He "will make [such a person] *a pillar* in the temple of My God" (Rev. 3:8-12, NASB). Those lives ordered by God's Word become like the pillars of Boaz and Yachin, upholding all that is unshakable. The Lord then promises to engrave upon those faithful believers "the name," the emblem of identity and authority, of what Hebrews announced as the believers' homeland: "the church of the firstborn," "the name of the city of My God, the New Jerusalem, which comes down out of heaven from My God, and My new name" (Rev. 3:12, NASB). Those faithful to "keep My Word" "will not go out from [the temple] anymore"

(Rev. 3:12, NASB)—they will be as unshakable as Boaz and Yachin.

The willingness, then, to have our steps ordered by the Lord determines whether we can stand in the new creation of an "unshakable" kingdom, or else will remain within that fallen cosmic order that He has promised to shake at its foundations. The remnant church must stand against apostasy by following an entirely different order than that of the fallen creation. It must stand corporately and individually as unshakable pillars, or else contribute even further to the apostasy of the world, sucked into the vortex of its disintegration and final collapse.

In Revelation, God's Word again connects the time of the apostatizing from God's covenant order to the dissolution of the cosmic order in the heavens: "I looked when He [the Lamb] opened the sixth seal, and behold, there was a great *earth*quake [the shaking on earth]; and the *sun* became *black as sackcloth* of hair, and the *moon* became *like blood*. And the *stars of heaven fell to the earth*, as a fig tree drops its late figs when it is *shaken* by a mighty wind [the shaking in heaven]. Then the sky receded as a scroll when it is rolled up, and every *mountain* and *island* was moved out of its place. And the kings of the *earth*, the great men, the rich men, the commanders, the mighty men, every slave and every free man, hid themselves in the caves and in the rocks of the mountains, and said to the mountains and rocks, 'Fall on us and hide us from the face of Him who sits on the throne and from the wrath of the Lamb! For the great day of His wrath has come, and who is able to stand?'" (Rev. 6:12-17). Here, again, the order of the earth is shaken, and then the order of the "sun" and the "moon" and the "stars" collapses until the whole of both falls in the forsaking of all faithfulness to God's covenant order (Matt. 24:5-30; Mark 13:5-26; Rev. 6:9-17).

The implications of this last point only emerge fully when we go back to the great prophetic description of the coming New Covenant in Jeremiah 31. There the prophet declares: "Thus says Yahweh, who gives the *sun* for a light by day, the ordinances of the *moon* and the *stars* for a light by night, who disturbs the sea, and its waves roar (Yahweh of hosts is His name): 'If those ordinances depart from before Me, says Yahweh, then *the seed of Israel shall also cease from being a nation* before Me *forever*'" (Jer. 31:35-36). It is this fixed order that is going to hold Israel together as an ordered community before God. Yet here in Revelation we see this fixed order collapsing. And we know how repeatedly God's Word tells us that the continued existence of His covenant people depends upon them not departing from the fixed ordinances of His commandments.*

---

* Jer. 31:35-36; 33:20-26; Matt. 24:29; Mark 13:24-26; Rev. 6:12-14; 8:12; Rev. 12:1-4.

Again, in the book of Revelation, in chapter 8, the seventh seal is opened: "Then the fourth angel sounded: And a third of the *sun* was struck, a third of the *moon*, and a third of the *stars*, so that a third of them were darkened. A third of the day did not shine, and likewise the night" (v. 12). Here we can begin to see that the book of Revelation is marked more by an overlaying template pattern than by a chronological pattern. Revelation 8 doesn't necessarily *chronologically* follow from Revelation 6 and 7. Rather, we see different templates, from different perspectives, laid over the same events, but all these templates reveal the same connection between apostasy and cosmic disorder followed by collapse (Matt. 24:5-30; Rev. 6:9-17).

We also see this same coming time of apostasy prophesied in 2 Thessalonians: "The mystery of lawlessness [disorder] is already at work; only He who now restrains will do so until He is taken out of the way" (2 Thess. 2:7). And we remember that in Matthew 24: "Because lawlessness [disorder] will abound, the love of most will grow cold" (Matt. 24:12, NKJV, NIV). Love is the content of God's purpose, but the temple order is the form that holds the content; and without that order, the content dissipates through the broken form of relationship and drains from human life. And so Mark 13 tells us: "Now brother will betray brother to death, and a father his child; and children will rise up against parents and cause them to be put to death" (Mark 13:12). Over and over the same motif is repeated: apostasy and disorder, followed by total collapse. What do we see here but a portrait of our own times, in the dissolution of families, the breakdown of marriages, men marrying men, women marrying women and the courts of the land upholding both?—the total inversion of the order of God.

Yet Revelation draws a great contrast when depicting the lives of those who keep *chesed*: "Here is the *perseverance* and the *faithfulness* of the saints" (Rev. 12:16–13:1, 6-7, 10, NASB, NIV). Again, the promise to those of the Philadelphian church to keep them unshakable during the time of trial that will come upon "the whole earth" is specifically addressed to those who keep His Word and who do not deny His name, His authority to order their relationships and lives in His Word and into His own identity. Against the backdrop of this dissolution of the final age, the breakdown of all covenant, of all relationships of love, with lawlessness and sin reigning and increasing, perseverance and faithfulness are called for. Now Boaz and Yachin must stand firm to uphold whatever they can continue to uphold of the order of God on this earth, "as it is in heaven."

In this postmodern age, the celebrated thinkers of the time are men like Michel Foucault, Jacques

Derrida and Richard Rorty, who proclaim that traditional morality, which to them smacks only of some obsolete standard, is an arbitrary imposition of what "ought to be" on what is.[6] So morality is seen as inherently evil, an attempt to force "reality" into a distorted mold. Morality and ethics in our day are despised and dismissed as "moralizing," "pietistic," "puritanical," "stodgy," "prudish," "repressed," "patriarchal." These are universally regarded—even by many professing believers—as bad things, ugly names now useful only to mock the ethic of God, an ethic through which He has reached to salvage from the debris of a collapsed culture a few souls clinging to the wreckage in the midst of the flood, the flood of the amoral and immoral. So the righteousness of God has been so smeared and contorted with the mud of corrupt minds that it is now made to appear as the face of evil. And the day is fast overtaking us when no one on earth will stand with those who uphold any standard—the latter will stand alone, as they did at the beginning. So if you do stand, you will soon feel as if you stand alone, and you will only be standing with God and those who are His.

When that time comes and the church is totally isolated in the eyes of the world, when it becomes the prey of every evildoer, soon the stars in the heavens will come down, because it truly is the same order that upholds the church that also upholds the firmament. And when that order has been willfully and totally rejected on earth, what purpose is there for it to remain in heaven (Gen. 1:14-19)? It is only this order on earth, of people giving themselves to the order of relationships and all else that God has commanded, that's holding back the cosmic collapse. But when that collapse comes, the new heavens and the new earth will then emerge (2 Pet. 3:13).

Of course, it is through "the blood of His cross" that God has "reconciled all things to Himself, . . . whether things on earth or things in heaven" (Col. 1:20), and it is given to the church to fill up His sufferings (2 Cor. 1:5-7; Col. 1:24). So it is through our submission to His sufferings, beginning with the crucifixion of our flesh and the breaking of our will to His will within His divine order, that we hold back chaos and destruction, the destruction that will finally close the door to the hope of redemption for fallen humanity. And it is through our continuing submission to this order, and to all through which the church must pass in this apostate age, that we will enter His resurrection and participate in the re-creation of a cosmos in perfect conformity to God's true nature of love.* Thus Paul explains: "For I consider that the sufferings of this present time are not worthy to be compared with the glory which shall be revealed in

---

* Rom. 8:18-25; 1 Cor. 15:51-55; 2 Pet. 3:10-13; Rev. 21:1-4.

us. For the earnest expectation of the creation eagerly waits for the revealing of the sons of God. For the creation was subjected to futility, not willingly, but because of Him who subjected it in hope; because the creation itself also will be delivered from the bondage of corruption *into the glorious liberty of the children of God*. For we know that the whole creation groans and labors with birth pangs together until now. Not only that, but we also who have the firstfruits of the Spirit, even we ourselves groan within ourselves, eagerly waiting for the adoption, the redemption of our body" (Rom. 8:18-23).

So our submission to this familial and church order is *not* peripheral. Indeed, from all that Scripture reveals, we can see that violation of this order in the New Testament church is incomparably more destructive than what Uzzah did when he put his hand to the Ark. When he presumptuously touched the Ark, he lost his life, halting for a time the return of the Ark to the place that God had ordained (2 Sam. 6:1-11; 1 Chron. 13:3-13). But now the church is fulfilling the actual, eternal purpose of which these Old Testament events were but the types and shadows.* We are entering the time of the culmination of all things. As Jeremiah said, the fixed order of the cosmos will stay in place as long as Israel is a nation before God.

---

* 1 Cor. 10:1-6, 11; Eph. 3:1-11; Col. 2:17; Heb. 8:5; 10:1.

Jesus and His apostles say over and over again that this fixed order will finally fall, and with it will fall the heavens.* Even the great cosmic bodies will fall from the skies. As Peter said, seeing what is coming, "What manner of persons ought you to be in holy conduct and godliness, looking for and hastening the coming of the day of God, because of which the heavens will be dissolved, being on fire, and the elements will melt with fervent heat? Nevertheless we, according to His promise, look for new heavens and a new earth in which righteousness dwells" (2 Pet. 3:11-13).

So God has given a definite order of covenant, of relationships built on *chesed*. To repeat, we are now in the midst of the age of apostasy, of divorce, of the breaking of the covenant order of God. And the most insidious aspect of this apostasy is that it's justified in the name of God and a cheap-grace salvation. For instance, the destruction of marriage is being fomented by those who claim to uphold marriage. Yet to say that two people of the same sex can form a marriage is the same as saying a rabbit is a lizard or a lizard a rabbit. You can call it that if you want to, but nothing is changed by this false label. In this apostatizing world of confusion, an incredible pull seeks to uproot us from all relationships of the kind of love that Ruth and Boaz exemplified. And if all that we have derived

---

*Matt. 24:29; Mark 13:24-25; Rev. 6:12-14; 8:10-12; 12:3-4.

from God's Word here is true, everything concerning the essential place of God's corporate order in the church and how we must uphold it and conform to it, then we must recognize that our adherence to these forms and patterns determines whether Jesus Christ is truly our Lord and our God. If that is the case, then the false christs that Jesus said are coming are false christianities and false churches that claim to come in His name while actually denying His Word and His authority, just as Jude warned (Jude 4, 8, 16-19). They are thus bringing the very apostasy and collapse that Revelation and the other New Testament scriptures warn is coming, with all the implications that we've seen this entails.

The Specificity of True Commitment

All such denials of the need to obey God in His Word and authority find a simple and direct scriptural refutation in the *chesed* of Ruth. Her life shows her genuine connection both to the God of Israel and to His people by showing how her acts of *chesed* honored God's covenant order. As we've begun to see, our place in this covenant order, as with Ruth, is not general, abstract or theoretical, but it comes through specific covenant relationships of *chesed*. These relationships join us to the comprehensive spiritual order of the Body of Christ as it fulfills its place in upholding the entire cosmic order of life. In Ruth's life, her *chesed* to her new husband Boaz and to her old mother-in-law Naomi also similarly brought her into her place in the greater order of Israel and Israel's transcendent purpose. So her relationship to her husband was actually subsumed in her larger relationship to the community of Israel.

In regard to her initial commitment, when Ruth spoke her vow, she did not then remain in Moab talking to Orpah and smiling in smug self-righteousness about how she was "mystically" joined to "mystical" Israel. Her joining entailed a very specific obligation and action in regard to a very specific person, Naomi. And she continued to serve Naomi as a daughter serves a mother. It was this *specific* fealty to her mother-in-law that evoked Boaz's praise and respect, only then leading on to further ways she would be joined to Israel through her *chesed*. Ruth did not merely enter into some vague and abstract context of the "universal" nation of Israel, only to then desert Naomi as if devotion to Naomi would hinder her loyalty to the more abstract covenant nation and so "divide" her from that nation. Ruth did not believe that she was now vaguely somehow joined to the people of God in a nebulous, abstract, intangible sense, which thereby released her from her concrete covenant obligation within the *specific* relationships in which God had placed her. Far from this, Ruth joined herself in a *specific* relationship with Naomi: "Where *you* go, I will go . . . ." And this relationship with Naomi is precisely what joined her to Israel, leading to her place in a *specific* part of the nation of Israel, a *specific* tribe, within a *specific* clan and a *specific* family and finally unto a *specific* man in her marriage to Boaz. In short, the fulfillment of her specific covenant obligation to one person could be said to have been the *only* thing that brought her into covenant with the larger community—not the other way around. As Dietrich Bonhoeffer said: "In your love you see only your two selves in the world, but in marriage you are a link in the chain of generations." So to Bonhoeffer, marriage was not merely a couple's "private possession," but it's something that "God causes to come and to pass away to His glory, and calls into His kingdom."[7] It's for His community. So, once again, this marriage between Boaz and Ruth shows that when the temple covenant with God and man is ordered right, it upholds the firmament, the very fixed order of God. And it further shows that one faithful man of *chesed* can be a link in the line that brings Messiah into the world.

Moreover, Boaz wasn't primarily the person of Ruth's natural choice but of God's choice and then Naomi's. If she'd made her own choice based on what was natural, she might have chosen to stay with

Orpah. Then she would never have been joined to Israel or to God, never coming under the wings of Yahweh's refuge. Furthermore, her covenant obligation joined her in these above *specific* ways and not simply *abstractly* to just any part of the people of Israel that *she* might for the moment choose, floating as a butterfly from one place to another, from one clique of scattered individuals to another, sharing no deep or enduring *life in God*. And notice that her specific commitment and "loyalty" to Naomi ("Where you go, I will go") did not "sever" her from Israel or Israel's God. Rather, it constituted her tangible expression of how real her devotion to God actually was, for Ruth then said, "*Your people* will be *my people* and *your* God my God."

To those few who might at this point desperately like to dismiss the (for them) uncomfortable example of Ruth as being merely "*Old* Testament," a question naturally arises: Are the spiritual relationships of God's people in the New Testament to be more superficial and ephemeral than those of the Old? The book of Hebrews, speaking of these Old Testament believers, declares, "These were all *commended* for their *faith*, yet none of them received what had been promised. God had planned *something better* for us so that only *together with us* would they be *made perfect*" (Heb. 11:39-40, NIV). "Something *better*" to a God who defines Himself as love (1 John 4:8, 16) must surely include deeper relationships than those that even Ruth, Naomi and Boaz could know, particularly since Jesus said that the depth of our relationships with one another would distinctively characterize His disciples: "I give you a *new* commandment: *love one another*; just as I have *loved* you, you also must *love one another. By this love* you have for one another, *everyone will know that you are My disciples*" (John 13:34-35, JB). So we are to love one another with the same love that He had for us—a love that bound Him both to us and to God even unto death, a redeeming covenantal love (Phil. 2:5-8; Heb. 10:5-7); and by this love people would know that we are His disciples. If someone admits, then, that we are to love God with New Covenant love, then Jesus here makes it plain that this is precisely the same kind of love we must show those to whom He directly joins us.

Herein lies the meaning of *chesed*: it defines our loyalty to *specific* obligations, "to the community in relation to relatives, friends, guests, master and servants" and so forth.[8] We have, in other words, *specific* covenantal functions, responsibilities, commitments and so on within specific covenantal relationships. We stand enduringly linked to *specific* people in *specific* ways, not merely abstractly and ephemerally to the "mystical" Body of Christ universally. Paul said that God has determined the bounds of our very habitations so that we might seek and find Him, though in

Him we live, move and have our being (Acts 17:26-28). In other words, living and moving and having our being in God doesn't mean that we've yet found or know God. Rather, it takes God's special arrangement of people and place to do that.

Nor does the fact that we're bound to this specific people imply in any way that we're separated from the larger Body. The fact that a cell is "specially" and permanently bound together to the other cells of, say, an arm, or of the lungs, does not "separate" it from the whole body. The very notion is absurd on the face of it. Rather, it is precisely by being joined in this enduring way that a cell is joined to the whole body. In short, our covenant with a particular body of believers, under the ministry that disciples that body, is *not counterposed* to our covenant with Christ and His universal Body, any more than a husband's and wife's separate covenant *within* their family separates them *from* that family, or any more than a family's own distinct covenant relationships separate them from the local body. Instead, as the apostle John makes explicitly clear, *it is through this particular covenant with specific brothers and sisters whom "we can see" that we are bound together with the universal Body of brothers and sisters whom we cannot see* (1 John 4:20).

In other words, an amorphous abstraction—"the mystical Body of Christ"—will not securely place us under the wings of heaven nor fasten our souls to the Father of us all. Rather, we are joined to Him through specific relationships with other men and women of flesh and blood, through the real *communion* of *participation* in the body of brothers and sisters whom "we can see," the Body of Christ as it still continues to come on earth in our human nature (2 John 7, Wms.).

In fact, the universal has no tangible meaning apart from the particulars that express it. It must be instantiated in the concrete. In fact, if all of us as finite human beings would take care of all the particulars that the eternal God has called us to, then the universal would take care of itself. *Chesed* is our faithful perseverance in the actual, concrete fulfillment of our particular commitments to God and to the specific community of brothers and sisters that "we can see," those with whom God has joined us through our spiritual birth into the kingdom to work out the tangible, day-to-day realities of covenant. *Chesed* is our "unity, solidarity, . . . lasting loyalty, faithfulness, . . . show [of] faithfulness, . . . individual acts flowing from solidarity."[9] *Chesed* is what fills up our lives to give meaning and fulfillment to the covenant vows we have made. It is the ongoing unfolding and fulfillment of, the fidelity to, the *b'rit*, the great covenant of God given us in the Body and blood of our Lord of covenantal love.

Chesed is often simply translated as "steadfast love"

or "covenant keeping." So a lack of *chesed* in our lives reveals a lack of authentic covenant, which reveals a lack of genuine love. This is true in spite of whatever initial ceremonies or sacraments we may have passed through or how much we may cling to some formal position of proximity to others in the Body. In such instances, covenant then becomes an empty face, a featureless mask, a hollow sham. For it is *chesed* that pours into the initiating of covenant, into the *form* of *b'rit*, its meaning and *content*.

What would it mean, for instance, to step to the altar and say, "From this time forth, and even forevermore," as we give our vows "before God in the sight of many witnesses," only to then—say, after three days, three months, three years or even three decades— desert or betray our spouse? Would it mean that, because we had once entered into the covenant, we could therefore claim to have stood forever as covenant-keepers, that we were forever a part of the covenant and could therefore never be viewed as apostate from it? No, it would mean exactly what it appears to mean: that we are hypocritical liars and covenant breakers, holding in contempt everything sacred. And in the case of our initial commitment to Christ, this contempt would include even the very blood of the New Covenant as Hebrews 10:29 tells us: "Of how much worse punishment, do you suppose, will he be thought worthy who has *trampled the Son of God underfoot, counted the blood of the covenant* by which he was sanctified *a common thing*, and insulted the Spirit of grace?"

Furthermore, we would have broken our vows before God because we would have broken *chesed*. We would have betrayed our obligations, our commitments. The same holds true of the Body of Christ: because we have made some empty confession doesn't mean in itself that we're actually part of His New Covenant; for as necessary as the making of the covenant is, the *realizing* and the *keeping* of the covenant prove even more necessary. Otherwise, the covenant vows have been rendered null and void—a vacuous sham. If you *ever* break them, then they are broken and remain so until you mend them. To say otherwise is mere mental sleight of hand—a theological flimflam.

The Mercy of Chesed

Those who abandon their covenant with God or God's people without a word of *honest* explanation, or only with the easy words of those who in their hearts or lives have gone through multiple divorces and remarriages, are no better than those who abandon their spouses, their children or their parents without a word of explanation or merely on the slightest or most perverted and selfish pretext—they simply have no love; it has been eaten up by their narcissistic souls. Theirs is the shallow soil never destined to experience the authentic and enduring love of God (Mark 4:5-6, 16-17). A brother, we are told, is made for adversity (Prov. 17:17). So if we fail in the day of adversity, then we have no strength (Prov. 24:10), no strength of love, which Solomon said is "as *strong as death*" (Song of Sol. 8:6-7). Of course, this love as strong as death, this redeeming love of God that promises to raise us from the dead, and that is the hope of our salvation, lies beyond our own ability to generate. Only God can give such love, but He gives it through the covenant and therefore in the context of the covenantal Body—the Body of the redeeming Christ (Song of Sol. 8:6).

Those who willfully break this covenant are not lost and wounded sheep but feral goats seeking only their own selfish desires and lusts. It is the church that is wounded by these faithless souls—it is the church that needs the Great Physician—not those shallow, untroubled souls who place such little value on their word, on love or on their covenant obligations before the God who is love. They value all these too little to even so much as offer a face-to-face explanation, either to the church or to other individuals crushed by their betrayal.

In many versions of the Old Testament, *chesed* is also translated as "*mercy*." Many have wondered why it would be translated this way. First, imagine that you were married (happily, you thought) for twenty years. You shared many experiences, many joys *and* sorrows, until the memories of these became the very substance of your life. Then one day you come home from work only to find that your spouse has betrayed or even abandoned you. What would that do to you? How would you feel if you found a note saying, "I haven't loved you for years—I may have never loved you. I've thought of leaving you many times before, and now I've finally taken the step. Don't bother trying to find me. The fewer 'good-byes' the better. It will save us all the pain." How would such a note affect you? How would you feel inside?

Or what if for years you had rejoiced and thanked God that you, of all the people that you knew, would never have to worry about *your* spouse's faithfulness? No matter what others might face or what you might face from others, *your* spouse was different, *your* spouse had integrity before God, *your* shared love was deep and true. What if you had with confidence built upon these assumptions until they had even gone far in defining who you were in the sense that you, at least in part, took your own measure by the depth, the loyalty and faithfulness that others, such as your spouse, felt toward you in your shared life as one? And what if, after all this, your world were shattered by the sudden knowledge that nothing was as it had seemed?

What if you actually discovered that this, or some similar, betrayal was long in the heart of your spouse, even if your beloved hadn't yet left you? What if you caught your spouse "making eyes" at someone else or even caught them in the arms of someone else; and this rank outsider to your marital covenant—a total stranger not only to you but also even to your spouse—had previously heard and even passed on to many others the word that your spouse was "on the make"? And what if many therefore had begun to know that your spouse was living on some level of unfaithfulness, that a covenant-breaking was imminent or had already occurred, and all that you were now waiting for was to discover when it had happened and with whom, or when it would take place or happen again? But you would now live constantly, every day of your life, under the threat of your life ripping asunder, or under the realization that your beloved, and even that love itself, were not what you had always held them in your heart to be, that to your spouse love was very small in contrast to what you thought the two of you had shared, what you thought was something deep and wondrous and untouchable.

Perhaps when caught in the betrayal, your spouse confessed that it was no deep feeling *against* you or *for* someone else that motivated the treachery, but simply a vain desire to prove that he or she was still attractive to the opposite sex. But then you would know that this is the same sort of vain selfishness that, in a time of crisis—say, an accident or a health crisis—reveals a love so shallow, so inturned, that the unfaithful spouse, instead of loving and caring for their sick or broken partner, is secretly wishing they'd go ahead and die so the unfaithful one can remarry and "start life again." So in the closing moments of your life, you feel your love and life have been utterly worthless to those you loved the most, that no one cares about your struggle with death and even would like to hurry it up and sweep you on into the grave. Perhaps the unfaithful spouse already, if even only in their minds, had been "shopping around," thinking about who would make a good replacement for the one who had loved her (or him) so deeply and given them their all, whose health had perhaps even broken in part because they *had* given everything.

Or what if your spouse's betrayal was with your best friend or your own natural brother, if you were a man, or with your best friend or your own natural sister, if you were a woman—the person you most trusted in the world next to your spouse? Your sense of betrayal would feel compounded almost beyond bearing.

In any of these scenarios, the world would become a different place for you, one where no one, not even those you loved the most, could be trusted. Your world would threaten to shrink to the tiny cell of your own pain and disconnectedness, your own sense of floundering incoherence; you would begin to struggle to overcome your disgust for yourself as someone worthy of such a betrayal, and you would also struggle against your mistrust of everyone else. You would look at people and fight the feeling that says, "I know what human beings are capable of—how can anyone dare to love in such a world?" If you were tenderhearted before, you would have to fight an entirely new perspective that now tempted you to harden your heart, as you tried to be invulnerable to the phoniness of so much that passes for love.

Nor am I writing here of imaginary instances. These very things have happened to people I know well. Many who read this will know of these specific instances, and I also know of specific instances exactly like these.

Even without the dread or threat of further betrayal, in such circumstances, your life as the betrayed would be shattered just to know that love was so much less than you had always believed, that trusts and confidences given and vulnerabilities made had merely exposed you to ridicule, to cruelty and mockery from the mouths of the heartless young and from ruthless, coarse adults who snickered and whispered to one another when you walked by. All through the infidelity of your spouse, because everyone knew it but you, your trust in love had made you to appear merely foolish in the eyes of all those with whom your beloved betrayed you.

For those who share nothing, give nothing of themselves, no such threats or feelings ever bother them. Yet for those who give everything, who become vulnerable and exposed only so they might share completely and totally without reserve, only so they might become absolutely one, such a threat wounds them deeply, sometimes unto death. Even if only a child or a parent betrayed the family in something of this way, it would shatter the other members if they had truly given themselves to the betrayer. (Some would, of course, call this "codependency," but this is just another word to justify the loveless life of people in an age that will no longer risk love, or abide by what they see as "outdated" covenant vows that interfere with their selfishness. These are people who don't really even care for or about one another.)

So in such a shattering circumstance, any peace and security you had found in living confidently in the faithfulness of love and with your beloved would now vanish. Your life would now be filled with the tension of potential further betrayal. You would no longer feel loved or cared for but alone and vulnerable in a hostile, uncaring world, while still feeling required to keep up appearances "for the sake of the children," or for some other social obligation. Yet every time your spouse left the house, a new fear and anxiety would take hold of you. Every encounter he or she had with the opposite sex would now be cause for apprehension—after all, your confidence in love had utterly fooled you once before. Every interest, every conversation would now be laden with the burden of possible betrayal. Life would become an agony of stress, pain, hurt, longing, loneliness, feelings of worthlessness. How, after all, could you be worth anything? —Just look at how the one you loved most in the world, and who claimed to love you most, treated you. (It is almost beyond belief that some loveless souls would actually use this kind of destructive anxiety against their spouse merely to elicit a little more personal attention from their now anxious and heart-weary mate.)

The opposite of such feelings of betrayal and infidelity comes with the absolute certainty that you can trust the one you stand in covenant with; and such absolute certainty comes only from knowing absolutely that your covenant partner is a person of *chesed*. So all this explains why to be a man or woman (or a God) of *chesed* is often translated in the Bible "*to be merciful.*" Because to trust the one you stand in covenant with fills you with great peace and serenity—even great courage. So it's an act of mercy on someone's part to stand faithful to the covenant they have made. And such faithfulness can hardly help but fill you with great gratitude.

The enduring words of Ruth, which formed the sanctions of her covenant, "The Lord do this to me and more also if aught but death separate me from thee," could be spoken with sincerity because she so completely trusted Naomi and Naomi's God. We may not express it as often as we should, but when we know with equal trust and certainty that we are bound to someone who holds faithfully to his or her covenant oath, no matter what, when not even a particle of doubt remains in our hearts or minds about the trustworthiness of this person, then surely they, by their character and lives, have shown a great mercy to us. Then we know that our covenant is such that our partner also trusts and knows where we stand, even though they may not acknowledge it like they should. Petty outward attentions and gifts seem trite and foolish compared to this underlying depth of love, a love that we can only feel when bound to someone who perseveres in unbending faithfulness to the covenant.

After all, have we not made the vow, and if we cannot trust each other in such a vow, then what meaning do the daily repetitions and petty tokens of love possess? When we break the vow, we have broken the form that holds all of this together and makes it all meaningful. Yes, a world of feeling can be conveyed in a word or even a look, but only when faithfulness to covenant carries the concrete specifics of the covenant's content. On the other hand, in an age of material abundance, the greatest of beneficent gestures simply slips away and falls to the ground, dissolving like ice on summer sidewalks, when the vow has been broken. Faithfulness to covenant brings great peace and security to our lives because covenant to God and to those who are His people is so great a thing, so binding a thing, so immutable. It unites people at the roots of their being, and the severance or even weakening of that bond inflicts the most terrible inner agony.

Please understand—I am not saying that a broken vow can never be mended. But when you have been made one with, surrendered the whole substance of yourself to, another person, their unfaithfulness cuts you to the core, it makes you feel as if part of your very self is falling away from you, like a broken, then severed wing, dangling and twisting in excruciating pain, then finally falling away. In the shattering of your shared identity with such a person, you feel diminished in what you are as a human being, almost unto death.

Love is admittedly a great risk, but the risk in attaining the fulfillment of the real thing is also so great that sincere people come to realize that only something as sacred and inviolable as a covenant with sanctions, something to be transgressed only with the most devastating consequences to human life, can protect us from the enormous risks to which our souls are daily exposed in such relationships. And that's precisely why God placed such heavy sanctions on vows.

The Courage to Be Vulnerable

Within the bounds of mutual love given in covenant commitment, we gain courage to open our hearts and make known our own deepest needs as we take responsibility for serving the needs of others. Such a life dedicated to love offers no alternative to vulnerability. After all, life is full of *unknowns*, and to open yourself up to what you do *not* know defines the very essence of vulnerability, of faith in God to lead you on your pilgrimage to a place of relationship you do not yet know, a land of uncertainties that constitutes your entire future life in Him (whether on earth or in heaven). A sacralized covenant is precisely what gives us the courage to become vulnerable in this way—the terms of the covenant with its commitment and faithfulness cover us in our inner exposure and vulnerability. And since all life faces unknowns that make us all vulnerable, covenant alone can cover the totality of life, even its unknowns. To enter covenant, then, means somehow finding the faith to totally trust not ultimately people but the God who puts people together to endure and prevail in love. And so this trust must also prevail, no matter how appearances may seem to dictate otherwise. This, in turn, means opening oneself, exposing oneself and thus becoming vulnerable to the vicissitudes of life and all its unknowns, which each and all of us must face. As said before, a covenant with sanctions not only binds us to something that remains in part unknown, but it commits us to fully lay bare the hidden essence of our inner self. Without each one revealing this essence of what he or she is, what hope can we have of that total and complete love that makes those two essences one (John 17:20-23)?

So we of the New Covenant admit our need of the service of others (1 Cor. 12:15-26; Gal. 5:13; 1 Pet. 4:10), and we also commit ourselves to serve others. Furthermore, we agree to serve them not just at our convenience; rather, we agree to pour out the substance of our lives into the covenant form, which promises to bring them the greatest possible joy, in the sense of the blessedness that comes only from the eternal God. We come into the deepest level of relationship because we admit that, merely within ourselves, we are incomplete and that we must depend in part on others in order for God to fully supply our own deepest needs (Eph. 4:16; 1 Cor. 12:20-25; 1 Pet. 4:10). This dependence, which begins with God but does not end there, includes love. We, in turn, will stand responsible to meet certain of their deepest needs (Gal. 6:2; 1 Pet. 4:10; James 1:27–2:17); and the motivating force of this service will not be external compulsion or any selfish incentive. Instead, it will be the pure, self-sacrificing and royal love of a God who incarnated His own life in a baby in a Bethlehem manger and then followed the constraints of this love from these humble beginnings to the bitterest and most humiliating of ends—all for the sake of others. So when we expose ourselves in this way, we feel, again, vulnerable—as naked as on a cross. Therefore when someone we love keeps covenant once they have entered into this raw level of relationship with us, it is, to repeat, a great mercy. This, again, explains why *chesed* is translated as "lovingkindness" and why we are told that God's "lovingkindness [*chesed*] is better than life."

Indeed, *chesed* is the most frequent term Scripture uses to characterize the nature of God's love: "His mercy," His *chesed*, "endures forever" (Ps. 136:1-26). In the Ten Commandments, in specifying the conditions of the covenant Yahweh made with Israel at Sinai, Yahweh declared of Himself that He shows "*chesed* to a thousand generations of those who love [Him] and keep [His] commandments" (Exod. 20:6,

NIV). He is a covenant-keeper, a faithful God who will not alter the words that He has uttered. He will forever stand by His Word (Isa. 55:11; Jer. 31:33-37; Matt. 24:35). And this provides for us great comfort and consolation, a mercy, because of, as said, our terrible vulnerability as creatures bound by and bound for death. So it is not something peripheral to our lives when He says, "I will never leave you nor forsake you" (Josh. 1:5).

The substance of *chesed* can be said to constitute the *deeds* and the *actions* of love itself (James 1:27–2:17). For so many, particularly in recent generations, love, like the kingdom of God, has been a "pie-in-the-sky-when-I-die" fantasy: it merely exists "somewhere up there," in our heads, in abstract dreams and romantic fairytales, even in phony visions expressed only in great empty gestures, usually trying to sell something. Such gestures never assume substance or become a reality because ours is a generation that increasingly lacks *chesed*. Ours has become, in fact, one of the saddest eras of history, an era increasingly marked by not only covenant-breaking but also covenant-hating (2 Tim. 3:1-9), where everything once sacred has now been desacralized and things once wondrous have been made dull and commonplace, or even a source of mockery and parody. This includes the relationship between men and women, which many people feel must be made more and more bizarre and kinky to compensate for less and less love. The jaded condition always pushing the limits leaves us in this wretched place. Because nothing transcends our own personal interests, which can only be satisfied but never fulfilled, we turn to perversity or romanticism—the latter projecting into tomorrow the fantasies we vainly hope will fulfill the reality of love we lack today. But what creates our lack is, again, that we can find nothing sacred, nothing to inspire a wonder and awe that takes us beyond our self-centered, tiny, empty worlds. Consumed with the supremacy of our pettiest selves, we have forgotten what it means to enter into and keep the covenant. This is simply because we have forgotten its value and purpose. We've also forgotten the dire results that naturally come from breaking any covenantal vow, a covenant with sanctions (Heb. 10:26-29; Acts 4:32–5:16).

Yet it is just when we wander without direction in these barbarous and merciless spiritual wastelands that God reveals the true meaning of His *chesed* to us in the life of someone who kept His word to the end, who "bore it out even to the edge of doom";[10] and upon Him was written a name, "Faithful and True" (Rev. 19:11). To glimpse that life is to stare into the battered but constant face of *chesed* (Isa. 52:14).

Covenant brings all our romantic notions, gestures, fantasies and vague professions of love and care out of the ethereal realm of abstraction down to the real world of the concrete. For instance, love between a man and woman (as distinct from merely lust) exists only in the mind until we enter into the bond of the marriage covenant. Then it exists in reality. Covenant brings all love out of all fantasy worlds, out of never-never land, an unattainable land always residing "somewhere over the rainbow." Covenant brings love down to the concrete world of people, place and time. It brings it out of the mind and into life. Covenant, not sentimental or romantic notions, makes love real, makes it more than self-centered fantasy or animal lust endlessly perverted, as if constantly poking at it to spark some movement of life, like a cat tossing around a dead mouse, trying to prod it back to life so it can continue to play with it. Covenant, in contrast, offers the reality within which love is truly tested. As said, only in covenant can it be determined whether love is as powerful and wonderful as those who seek it have supposed it to be. Only through covenant can we prove whether it has the power to overcome and prevail in the everyday life of what is (often even without irony) called the "*real* world."

That is what *chesed* is: it is the durableness of love, love's enduring power over the duration of the fullness of our time on earth. And that concrete evidence must be lived out in real actions and situations, in specific places and localities, with real people. It must take place in the context of enduring, exclusive covenant relations with those specific people in those specific places, people to whom we have faithfully committed ourselves and whom we self-sacrificially serve. This self-sacrificial service is what sacralizes our lives and gives them meaning: we serve others because we stand in awe of who God made them to be and of whatever it is that causes them, against all odds, to continue growing into His image; we serve them because we stand in awe of what God did to bring that image to life in them. To suddenly stand in awe of what was at one time in our lives deemed the merely commonplace is to transform life into the mystery of God. It makes of life a living wonder.

We can only avoid the pitfalls pulling us into greater miseries by maintaining our vision of life as a mystery. All truth—as the Greek word for truth, *aletheia*, which literally means "unconcealment," suggests—is unveiled to us only as we discern it unfolding out of this mystery. We must recognize that truth is something revealed to us, disclosed to us—not something created or invented by us, as is popularly supposed—and that without this supernatural disclosure it remains forever hidden. So we can't cavalierly shoulder our way through life assuming we know everything, mainly because we certainly don't, and can't. Only the smugness and complacency of an arrogant pride, which more than anything blinds us to the truths hidden in the mystery of life, convinces us that we know everything we need to know in order to successfully and fully live life. But life has a way of showing us that it's much bigger not only than we thought but also bigger than we ever imagined.

A wife wrote once to her husband, after nearly 40 years of marriage: "Your love means life to me, but I realize now that I don't understand your love because I've come to realize I don't understand you." She was confessing her realization that life and people are such a mystery that we can't understand them, at least not in the sense of comprehending them by placing them under the microscopes of our intellects. We're always dealing with worlds that are unfathomable to us because the vast and eternal God of a vast and eternal love is passing through those worlds, a God whom we do not always see in the circumstances of life (Job 9:11). This is the God who wants to reveal Himself to and through us in all these circumstances.

So this isn't a mystery rooted in pride, where we try to make ourselves interesting and attractive to others by being "mysterious," or where we try to circumvent our accountability to God by making Him so mysterious and unknowable that we are left to be the god of our own lives. Rather, this is a mystery rooted in humility, where we're humbled by the very knowable, concrete acts of love and goodness that come our way when we don't deserve them. This, in short, is a mystery rooted in awe of the observable love and wisdom of God. This is why Paul declared, "Oh, the depth of the riches both of the wisdom and knowledge of God! How unsearchable are His judgments and His ways past finding out!" (Rom. 11:33).

So love is too big for us to cram into the thimbles of our minds. Life is also too big for that. And so God is also too big for us to contain Him in our thoughts and plans. That's why it's so wrong to abstract little pieces or segments of someone's life and then characterize the whole person by that selected piece or segment. "Don't you remember when so-and-so did that terrible thing?" someone says to us. "When was that?" you respond anxiously. "Oh, it was 45 years ago," they say. "How long did that go on?" you ask. "Six months," they reply. And so that's what this "offending" person became for the rest of his entire life—just what he did for 6 months, 45 years ago! That failure of six months out of an entire life has confined the other 70 years to failure. That's often the way things seem to happen, though, isn't it? The world strikes out and assigns identities to people on the basis of the lowest, weakest, most superficial and unrepresentative moments in their lives. It is always reducing people to pinpoint bull's-eyes made up of their worst moments, targets that can be shot at and destroyed, often from no other motive than sheer envy, jealousy and meanness.

How opposite is God's view, though—"Oh, how unsearchable are the judgments of God and His ways past finding out." And this is the case because He puts all these isolated moments in a larger context; and the larger the context gets, the more that moment changes into something entirely different than it seemed to be at the beginning. It soon becomes, as my grandmother (who was an artist) once told me, only a dark background shadow adding depth to the character portrait of the person's luminous life. But those moving and skittering across the surface see only the isolated spot, the minute fact, the single failure. And that's what's then pulled out and displayed as a target for every passing gossip to shoot his tongue at.

"How unsearchable are the judgments of God and His ways past finding out"—because He's bringing people together in a different kind of knowledge than facts and tidbits and pinpoint failures. He's bringing them together in the relational knowledge of a love that's constantly expanding into the wholeness of God's own life and reaching beyond all failure. And instead of judging on the basis of one select and negative fact, pulled out of the whole context of someone's life, forgiveness targets even that failure; and, when that failure comes to repentance, forgiveness diffuses it until it becomes the background giving depth to a much bigger picture. So the life also becomes different than it was before. Love begins to grow, and the picture gets bigger and bigger until love assumes features, and then suddenly God's passing by and we *do* see Him (Job 9:11). We realize who was enlarging this picture, who was making it more than detailed points of guilt or innocence. It was a God of love: "No one has seen God at any time. If we love one another, God abides in us, and His love is being perfected in us" (1 John 4:12). Again, He's no longer just passing by, but He's there with us, in us and through us, and we want to abide in His love.

So the picture enlarges until God becomes a reality in human lives. Hate always reduces the whole of a person or people to a few discrete and often distorted facts, an area small enough for a tight shot-group on the pop-up target for the arrows of gossip. But love expands and enlarges human lives, binding people together into the larger image of their commingled lives—the image of God. Paul asked who can ever separate us from the love of this God who is in Christ Jesus (Rom. 8:35-39). It grows greater and greater, and the ties get stronger and stronger. "Great is the mystery of godliness: God was manifested in the flesh" (1 Tim 3:16).

And it's amazing to look back over a life and see

how, from our perspective *now*, God worked in that life in ways not seen at the time. God poured through the person's life, but the person didn't see it till later. And that manifestation of God in human flesh will keep growing until we see God face to face.

Judgment, on the other hand, always reduces. So you must not judge lest you be judged, lest you be reduced to *your* own worst elements, because judging others always narrows us down. But love always expands, always reveals more of itself and others, always manifests more of itself and releases others to do so, too. That's why God speaks to us so directly in the context of His covenant Body about our needs, so forthrightly—because He sees that otherwise, unless He does speak, we're going to believe and accept something that's too narrow about ourselves, about life, about others. And that narrowed vision will change us into an image that's not of God, that's too small for the bigness of God's love. So God pierces and cuts those things with His Word, brings repentance, then diffuses them with forgiveness and mercy because He doesn't want us to be caught by our own narrow and faulty images of ourselves or of others. He doesn't want us to get caught in a narrowed vision that destroys the image of God in human lives.

OUR DEBT OF LOVE

Since it must take place *in a place*, in a relationship, in a relational situation, covenant love proves confining and limiting to the baser, selfish nature, although few things in this world so liberate the human spirit. Yet as confining as place appears, to not know our place is by definition to be lost. To be in relationship to someone means to be conjoined to them according to a certain situation with certain coordinates—that is, we see them from a certain angle or position based on our situation in regard to them, whether as spouse, brother, sister, parent, child, employer, doctor, lawyer, governor or so on. All of this necessitates the specifics of finding our place in a definitive *order* of relationships. No one can serve *all* the needs of their own entire life by themselves. So we come to know each other through the way in which *we* can and do serve one another. By remaining faithful to that form of relationship through which we are bound to someone, by serving the grace of God through that form, we keep *chesed*. If we have not found our place in love, we fail to fully know our relationship to either the God who is love or to other human beings, and so, again, how can we be designated as anything but lost?

After all, this disorientation describes the very essence of being lost—the inability to find one's place. Where, then, is our home? Where is our place? What is the proper order and arrangement of our relationships and of our love service to one another? For Christians, when we have found that order of familial and community relationships in love, we shall have found our ultimate home—Jerusalem, the "city of peace" whose geography is not natural but spiritual. And the keeping of *chesed* is what will help us to answer all these above questions—it brings us out of the world of make-believe and down to the place of community and commitment. It brings us home. It is then, when we find our place, that we are found.

That is what Jesus meant when He said that "whoever wants to save his life will lose it" (Matt. 16:25, NIV). For unless, through *chesed*, we willingly give up our lapsed lives and all the images of ourselves, we can never find the place called "home"—we will always remain lost. When, however, we willingly lose our life, pour it out as a sacrifice in *that* temple in *that* Jerusalem (Rom. 12:1-3)—where time, place and the order of relationships are defined by God and therefore can put limitations on lapsed and irresponsible human conduct—that community in which, and in the midst of those people among whom, God has settled us, then we will find our true life in the culture that sustains life (Matt. 10:38-39). This is our place in the Body of Christ, in the kingdom of God, in the community of life; this is the home from which we were lost. In our marriage *to* Him, we find our identity *in* Him. This, too, is the meaning of *chesed*. *Chesed* is the making of commitments and obligations to God and the particular people who belong to Him, then keeping those commitments in place, in time—no matter what the cost or how much the hurt.

To understand the nature of *chesed* further helps us see, too, why the Hebrew Scriptures mandate such severe sanctions against those who enter the *b'rit* but fail to keep it. One part of the reason for such sanctions focuses on how covenant joins us to a great chain of life. This is an interlinked series of relationships joined at each link by commitment to a continual, intergenerational and faithful love in the service of a larger transcending community. When one link snaps, the whole chain breaks. So it is a terrible thing in the sight of God to break covenant, whether with our parents, with our spouse, with our children, with the Body of Christ or, what usually precedes all these other betrayals, with the Source of it all—God. Peter said it is better never to have known the way of righteousness than to enter it and then betray it (2 Pet. 2:20-21). And the more we come to know, the deeper we enter into *chesed*. And so the more God reveals, the more responsible we will be held for what we know. Therefore Jesus said,

"And that servant who knew his master's will, and did not prepare himself or do according to his will, shall be beaten with many stripes. But he who did not know, yet committed things deserving of stripes, shall be beaten with few. For everyone to whom much is given, from him much will be required; and to whom much has been committed, of him they will ask the more" (Luke 12:47-48). And so also the author of Hebrews warns us: "If we *deliberately* keep on sinning *after we have received the knowledge of the truth*, no sacrifice for sins is left, but only a fearful expectation of judgment and of raging fire that will consume the enemies of God. Anyone who rejected the law of Moses died without mercy on the testimony of two or three witnesses. How much more severely do you think a man deserves to be punished who has trampled the Son of God under foot, *who has treated as an unholy thing the blood of the covenant that sanctified him, and who has insulted the Spirit of grace?*" (Heb. 10:26-29, NIV). If we "receive the knowledge of the truth," if we experience and taste the depths and riches of the reality of God's covenant love, if we've claimed our will to be perfect in its commitment of our fallen nature into Jesus' sacrificial death, but then we *willfully* turn aside from that love and commitment, we declare that Jesus' sacrifice was nothing, was even despicable, that His love is a debased and worthless thing. If we sin willfully and knowingly against the grace of God, rejecting and despising that grace coming to us through Christ's Body, then we willfully reject even the possibility of our salvation.

Paul said in the fourteenth chapter of Romans that the day will come when we shall stand before God and *give account* for the things that we have done. This judgment will be in accordance with all that He has given us (Rom. 2:5-11; 14:10-12). This also sheds light on the meaning of *chesed*: to give, but not just in the sense of returning what has been given; if that is all we do, then we are, according to Jesus, "*unprofitable* servants" (Luke 17:10). If that is all, then we've only done what it was our *duty* to do, and when we only give in return for what has been given to us, no profit comes with that.

Those who put savings in the bank expect to draw interest from it. Anyone—it little matters how liberal or conservative—who invests money over a lifetime, in hopes that it will provide some security in old age when they can no longer work, would be furious to discover that their lifetime investment had failed, losing money instead of gaining it. This is the meaning behind the parable of the master who had given talents to his servants. One had increased what was given to him tenfold and another fivefold. But the third servant had merely hidden his talent and given back exactly what he had received. The master was furious and took and bound that "wicked and lazy" servant and cast him into the outer darkness where there was weeping and gnashing of teeth (Matt. 25:14-30). In talents, faith, gifts and love, God has invested something in us, and He will one day audit our account. John's Apocalypse also confirms that the day will come when the books will be opened, and we shall give an *account* of everything God has given to us (Rev. 20:12). So it seems we must become people who recognize this accountability, this liability, and so become reliable (from *ligare*, the root of the words *ligament*—see Eph. 4:16, NIV—and *religion*). We must, in short, become bound to our place of service in the *chesed* of covenant fulfillment.

For us, too, it will not suffice to merely return what we've received. And what is the "profit" that God wants? Without *love*, Paul wrote, "it *profits* [you] nothing" (1 Cor. 13:3). *Chesed* is the "steadfast love" that brings "profit" because *chesed* is what makes us give above and beyond what it is our duty to give (Luke 17:10; 2 Cor. 8:1-3). It does not merely return what has been given, but goes beyond and brings the "profit" of love, the only profit God's interested in. *Chesed* is what makes us give until our relationships are sacralized, a word that shares the same root with sacred and sacrifice. This love becomes our worship, our sacrifice, unto God (Rom. 12:1-3). Only in this sacrifice do we find the blessing that brings fulfillment to our lives because, as it is written, "it is more blessed to give than to receive." *Chesed* characterizes those who serve and give of themselves for the best interest and highest joy of those with whom they stand in covenant, even when it means sacrificing their own image, comfort, convenience, interests and life. They live, in short, for love. In a world of greed and selfishness, only the same *chesed* of the One who laid down His life for His friends can enable us to do that.

So God requires something of us. Paul proclaimed that we are not to look after merely our own interests, but also after the interests of others (Phil. 2:4). We are to owe no man anything except love (Rom. 13:8, KJV). But we do have an obligation to love—we "owe" it. We owe it, because this is all the "profit" from life that any of us will ultimately possess when we depart this world. And that obligation to love is our *chesed*. So we have a commandment from God to love one another, to love those to whom we are bound in the brotherhood of God's covenant (John 13:34): "Greater love hath no man than this, that a man lay down his life for his friends" (John 15:13, KJV). "Jesus Christ laid down His life for us," John said, "and we *ought to* lay down our lives for our brothers" (1 John 3:16). Again and again, we are shown to *owe* this love. It is a "debt" that God *requires* us to repay, and so He *commands* us to "love one another" (John 15:12, KJV). He can do so because He has invested us with this love by His own Holy Spirit (Rom. 5:5), and so He will one day bring us into account for our use of His investment. We shall be audited according only to our love (Matt. 25:31-46), against which there is no law (Gal. 5:22-23).

AN ACTIVE LOVE

Some scholars dispute the meaning of the word *chesed*. One side sees it as a purely obligatory commitment, the other as purely an expression of voluntary love. Both see only part of the truth. Covenant with God is a purely voluntary relationship motivated by love, but it is a love that has been *given* to us, which, because we have received it, we in turn now "owe," as Paul unambiguously insisted (Rom. 13:8). It is a grace, but by that grace we "work out" our salvation (Phil. 2:12-13), we "labor to enter His rest" (Heb. 4:9-11, KJV), we work at learning to love, which is the message carried by every marriage. This is a love that compels us to make the commitments, the specific, ongoing commitments, that covenant entails, and then to keep these commitments because of the love that continues to consume us (2 Cor. 5:14). *Chesed* includes both the voluntary love relationship and the *obligatory* covenant commitments that come with the *voluntary* giving of ourselves to the covenant. So Paul declares himself to be a "*debtor*" to everyone, "to the Greek, and to the Barbarian" (Rom. 1:14, KJV). His words show that our *chesed* obligation extends even to those outside the household of faith. This is because Messiah laid down His life for us, filled us with His love and commands us to love those who have not found their "place," a place in which they, too, can live out *chesed*. They are still in exile and lost in the wilderness outside God's love. We must seek to open our place, our "home," to them, whether they recognize love as their home or not. On the basis of our common *humanity* with all people, we have an obligation to serve God's love to our fellow man, and this apart from any reciprocation from them. But beyond this, we have an obligation of *chesed* that is due our commingled life, a *chesed* that is due to those *within* the kingdom of God. We've entered the blood covenant of Christ to give ourselves for our *brothers* (1 John 3:16). So we *owe* love to one another, a great love, a self-sacrificing love. We have an obligation, a "debt," an "account" that must be settled. And it will not do to be an "unprofitable servant" in the meeting of this obligation, our *obligation* to serve *in love* (Luke 17:10; Gal 5:13; Rom. 13:8). Yes, Jesus paid the full price, but we avail ourselves of what He did only if we're *in* Him—only if we've sacrificed our own fallen nature and thus entered His sacrificial atonement.

Chesed, then, describes the ability to follow

through, the ability to endure. It is the ability to bear out the covenant, as said, "even to the edge of doom." Jesus said that "they that *endure to the end*," those who prove the enduring power of God's love, those who keep their covenant unto death—even while the love of most "waxes cold" (Matt. 24:12-13, KJV)—they alone "shall be saved" (Matt. 10:22, KJV). "Be thou *faithful* even *unto death*," John wrote, and the Lord shall "give you a crown of life" (Rev. 2:10, KJV, NIV). So we must keep *chesed* even unto death. "Lo," Jesus said, "I am with you always, even unto the *end* of the world" (Matt. 28:20, KJV). *Chesed* displays a love powerful enough to reach the extremities of life and still prevail. But Jesus will stand faithful and true to everything He has spoken. He will keep *chesed*. He has given His life to prove it. Who can give more? What greater proof can we hope to find?

So now *we* must also be faithful and true, since covenant involves at least *two* faithful parties. The covenant stands conditional upon our *chesed*, our ability to bring our love obligations to completion, to realization, to follow through on our pledges, our obligations, on what we owe. We owe much because we were bought with a price, and we are not our own (1 Cor. 6:19-20). We owe, in fact, everything, our very lives, in love (Luke 9:23-25; 14:26-33; Rom. 12:1). This constitutes the nature of true service, of our true serving of the gifts of God, the sacrifice of our very lives. So Jesus said that we must pick up our cross and follow Him, follow Him on the path even as it leads through sacrifice, through suffering, to the laying down of our lives—follow Him unto death—because in *that* death resides the triumph over death and over him who has the power of death (Heb. 2:14-15; Eph. 2:1-3; 1 John 5:19).

So *chesed* is impelled by a selfless love pouring itself out completely in service. It goes, however, beyond mere obligation or "duty"—as said, it reaches out and will not give up until it attains to what is best for the one with whom we stand in covenant, the one we love. In short, it seeks to pour itself out in giving the very best it can give. God, we are told, refuses second-rate sacrifices (Mal. 1:13-14). He shuts the door of His temple to blemished rams (Mal. 1:10, 13-14). He accepts only *chesed*, *chesed* which impels us to give until our sacrifice of service attains to the highest we *can* give, until we withhold nothing, until we have no more to give. And when we have given all, then nothing remains to withhold, nothing that would prevent us from becoming one with the God who robed Himself in flesh and gave everything.

Only then can we hope to become one with each other. Nothing is held back from God or our brothers and sisters, and so our identities merge as one, and only then will they do so. The love of *chesed* alone can constrain us to do this. The power of this *chesed* can only abide in our lives through the renewing of our minds, the perpetual renewing of our covenant as we offer ourselves continually as living sacrifices unto the Lord (Rom. 12:1-2). And even then, we must still receive the power of the great *Chesed*-Keeper, the power of His Spirit.

Apart from God, we do not have the enduring power of *chesed* within ourselves. Like every other "good and perfect gift," it, too, "is from above" (James 1:17, NIV). Yet we must actively seek it in order to find it (Jer. 29:13; Matt. 7:7-8, Ampl.). Then, when it comes, we must receive it and give ourselves to it completely, holding nothing back. For, again, only this keeping of the covenant makes meaningful the entering of the covenant. In fact, it will ultimately determine our eternal fate.

It is a tragic delusion to think that because we have merely entered into the covenant we have therefore fulfilled all obligations of covenant. But we can actually break covenant in two ways. One is an open disavowal. The other comes merely by default, through our "neglect" of "so great a salvation" (Heb. 2:3). We treat it as something despicable, worth less than a bowl of soup. And then, like Esau, we cannot find a *"place* of repentance"—*a context of viable covenant relationships* with real people to work out and fulfill God's love—even though we may seek it diligently with tears (Heb. 6:4-8; 12:17). We cannot find this place because our love is too weak to propel us out of the comfort zones of the flesh to which we must die—we love our flesh too much and God too little.

And so all it takes to end up here is neglect (Heb. 2:3). What Jesus called a "wicked and lazy servant" hid his talent in his sweatband and buried it. He simply neglected it. When the Lord came and required it of him, his neglect cost him his soul (Matt. 25:24-30). So we have a further obligation—to fulfill, to make full, the content, the form, of the covenant that we pledged to fill with the sacrifice, the libation, of continually pouring out ourselves before God, the sacrifice of ourselves in love service to others (Rom. 12:1-3).

When he introduces to his readers the gifts that come when believers keep *chesed*, such as serving, giving, leading, *showing mercy* (Rom. 12:7-8), Paul exhorts them, "In view of God's *mercy*, to offer your bodies as living sacrifices, holy and pleasing to God—this is your spiritual act of worship" (Rom. 12:1, NIV). The covenant delineates a specific form that limits us and obligates us, and in remaining faithful to those obligations, we fulfill that form. If, however, we neglect the covenant, if we offer second-rate sacrifices (Mal. 1:6-14), then how shall we escape the black-hole pull of our selfish and corrupt nature? If we neglect the covenant, we merely deceive ourselves when we claim to keep it. It takes *chesed* to keep the covenant, to enable us to be the *diakonos* (the servanthood) God has called us to be. So nothing short of a complete *chesed* will do.

Jesus said he who is faithful in a very little thing is faithful also in much, and he who is unrighteous in a very little thing is unrighteous also in much: "If therefore you have not been faithful in the use of unrighteous mammon, who will entrust the true riches to you? And if you have not been faithful in the use of that which is another's, who will give you that which is your own? No servant can serve two masters; for either he will hate the one, and love the other, or else he will be devoted to one, and despise the other. You cannot serve God and mammon" (Luke 16:11-13, NASB). Neither can we serve both ourselves and God. Thus Jesus said that unless we "deny" ourselves, we "cannot be" His disciples (Luke 9:23; 14:27). If we would give ourselves in true love service, *chesed* must permeate *every* aspect of our lives. It must be the ruling principle in every action and word.

Through Zechariah, God admonished His people not to neglect "the day of small things" (Zech. 4:10). And elsewhere He warned that the "little foxes spoil the vine" (Song of Sol. 2:15). To despise the "small things" God has presently placed in our hands is to also despise in our hearts the great things God *would* do. The prophets declared that God's "people are destroyed for lack of knowledge" (Hos. 4:6). To ignore or neglect the covenant of God means we lack knowledge of it, we are ignorant of the covenant. And so we are destroyed as we stand outside God's covenant provision. As shown earlier, it is only within the confines of the covenant that anyone can fully *know* God. God's people are "called, chosen and faithful" (Rev. 17:14), and the word in Genesis 18:19 translated as "chosen"—"Abraham have I *chosen*"—can also be translated as "known." The Lord "knows those who are His," and those He knows therefore stand upon a sure foundation (2 Tim. 2:19, KJV). To be known by God is to be implanted with His saving grace, established within the context of the covenant. Yet those chosen must also remain faithful (1 Cor. 4:2; Rev. 17:14). They must keep *chesed* in every aspect of their lives, keeping faithful even in the seemingly minor details of their service. They must remain faithful in not despising the day of "small things" (Zech. 4:10).

Chesed doesn't merely passively acquiesce; it actively participates. It calls for taking initiative in doing good. If it were merely a matter of passively receiving what God gives, then the man who took and hid his talent in his sweatband, only to then bury it, would have been saved. But he was not saved, because he took no initiative (Matt. 25:24-30).* *Chesed* is

---

* See *Eternal Security* (1991, 2002) by Blair Adams and Joel

not a passive thing; it is faith motivated—moved to action by love (Gal. 5:6). It, therefore, expresses itself in deeds and acts (James 2:17-18, 20-22). Whatever motivates us propels us into action, into motion; and love is the motivation that holds us to what we love and moves us along in the spiritual dance with those we love. *Chesed* (as distinct from the motions of the flesh or human will) takes initiative as grace stirs the soul and the person responds. It moves forward in the circle of faithful relationships, a circle turning like a wheel under the pressure of a working grace, taking us forward toward our destiny in love.

All this necessitates bringing everything in our lives under God's dominion. This is how we participate in the kingdom of God, in the dominion of the King whom we have confessed as our Lord. To take no initiative toward this goal is to become an "unprofitable servant" (Luke 17:10), a servant whose faith is dead and therefore useless (James 2:14-17, 20, 26). Such people do not truly serve in love, because they do not truly care for or look after the needs

---

Stein and The Minister's Dialectical Handbook of Theology and Doctrine *On Atonement, Justification and the Law, Book Two: Justification* (1996, 2005) by Blair Adams (Elm Mott, Tex.: Colloquium Press) for a refutation of the notions of "once saved, always saved" and of the false dichotomy of grace and works and other related doctrinal errors. See also *Human Choice or Predestination?* by Blair Adams (Elm Mott, Tex.: Colloquium Press, 1986, 2003, 2008).

of those whom they serve. They must be told every detail of what to do in their service. Their service may be obligatory, but it is *merely* obligatory; so it never meets the greatest obligation, the obligation to love.

Matthew wrote these words: "At that time Jesus went on the Sabbath through the grain fields, and His disciples became hungry and began to pick the heads of grain and eat. But when the Pharisees saw it, they said to Him, 'Behold, Your disciples do what is not lawful to do on a sabbath.' But He said to them, 'Have you not read what David did, when he became hungry, he and his companions; how he entered the house of God, and they ate the consecrated bread, which was not lawful for him to eat, nor for those with him, but for the priests alone? Or have you not read in the Law, that on the Sabbath the priests [who *serve*] in the temple break the Sabbath, and are innocent? But I say to you, that something greater than the temple is here. But if you had known what this means, "*I desire compassion, and not a sacrifice*," you would not have condemned the innocent'" (Matt. 12:1-7, NASB).

Jesus here quotes from the Old Testament (Hosea 6:6). The word translated here as "compassion" is the word *chesed* in Hosea. And what was it the disciples were doing that required compassion (*chesed*), not sacrifice? Well, Jesus implicitly describes them serving in the temple—working for the Lord. It wasn't any *b'rit* ritual that had just brought them into the covenant. Now they were keeping *chesed*. They were meeting their obligations. They were serving the Lord. They had compassion, "feeling with" God and man. They were fulfilling both covenant service and covenant obligation in God's new temple.* They were not giving a sacrifice that substituted for the giving of themselves, but were wholly giving themselves because "sacrifice and burnt offerings I have not desired, but a *body* I have prepared. Here I am, I have come to do *Your will*." Or, as John wrote: "And I saw the dead, great and small, standing before the throne, and books were opened; and another book was opened, which is the book of life; and *the dead were judged* from the things which were written in the books *according to* [not their faith without works, their theology, their affections, their feelings, their emotions, but according to] *their deeds*" (Rev. 20:12, NIV, NASB). We will be judged according to our *deeds*,† the *reality* of our love made manifest, of our faith made perfect (James 2:21-22, KJV), of the *doing* of the covenant—our *chesed*, the faithful fulfillment of our commitment to serve in the "works" of faith (James 2:14-18; Eph. 2:10).

Again, this is the ability to follow through, to find

---

* See *An Introduction to the Temple and Its Foundation* by Blair Adams (Elm Mott, Tex.: Colloquium Press, 1983, 1988).

† See *Eternal Security* for refutation of the notion that this judgment only concerns our status in heaven and not our salvation.

our place, the specific place that God has ordained for us in His covenant Body, in His prescribed order of love service, and to stand in that place. When we first enter the *b'rit*, we speak our vow of commitment, but then we must enter into *chesed*, the actual keeping of the vow that conforms our life to the image of God's Son (Rom. 8:29). That is, we must *fulfill* the covenant, the commitments, the obligations that we have made, sacrificing ourselves to fulfill God's purpose. So it's true that we need to speak the words of *b'rit*, but then we must stand by them in *chesed*. That, then, is what defines *chesed*—standing by our word with our very life, standing by what we have proclaimed to be our freely given and heartfelt choice, faithfully fulfilling our place of covenant service, assuming our place and then taking our stand in it as we live out its obligations of love, becoming pillars in the temple of God.

CHESED AND WORDS TO STAND BY

Anyone who cannot honestly confess to wanting more than some momentary satisfaction will not, of course, ever sincerely enter any lifelong covenant. The insincere may be willing merely to mumble words in a meaningless public confession. But the avowal will probably never even enter their minds when it comes to confirming any substantive words in their daily conduct, much less in an entire life. Words that cannot be confirmed in actions or conduct or character are words, in the Biblical idiom, "not . . . mixed with faith" (Heb. 4:2, KJV). The Bible says this because in its viewpoint, as James wrote, professed faith without action is "dead" faith (James 2:20). So such words are really faithless words, words without conviction, empty words from hollow people who have no substance of character. These words without faithful actions "profit" people "nothing" (Heb. 4:2; 1 Cor. 13:1-3), for that real love which alone brings profit must act and live out its core impulse. God will find a faithful people who can mix His words, the words that He speaks to them, with faith. Then the reality of covenant love will manifest itself in the works of God that have been finished from the foundation of the world but are yet to be made manifest in this last time (Heb. 4:3; Eph. 1:10 with 2:10).

Paul wrote of the manifold wisdom of God, which will be *made known* to the angels and the principalities and the powers. This is the wisdom that God will manifest in and through the church in this last day in "the dispensation of the fullness of time," when He brings all things together that are in Christ, even together in Him (Eph. 1:10). God will find a people who will know that His words are not empty words merely to temporarily salve their consciences or prod their flesh out of slumber for a moment, empty words to temporarily sate them with some vague and fleeting sense of pleasure or even blessing.

And that is what satisfaction means: pouring everything in sight—both good and bad—into a bag with holes (Hag. 1:6, KJV). Satisfaction's bag must constantly return and be refilled, but the covenant is constituted of words that come forth with a view toward endurance, and therefore they are words that can be stood by for a lifetime. Such a covenant confession declares, "I speak these words; I stand by these words; I give myself to these words; I give answer to the call of my destiny from a good conscience by *saying*, 'Yes, I will, I do, and that unto death. I give myself until these words are *fulfilled* in *my* life. And I am determined to remain faithful to God until He re-creates me into someone who can live up to these words.'"

Fulfillment is a word suggesting something only covenant can bring, a word whose meaning implies a vow made in an authentic covenant unto God, in the joining of oneself to Him or to others in Him. Fulfillment does not come with cheap and empty words of lust and desire, of vain ambition and cheap grace poured into perforated bags. These always and constantly require bringing back the bag and muttering, "Fill it up again, please—I'm no longer satisfied with what I had before." Wendell Berry is the source of insight into the difference between satisfaction and fulfillment. In quoting Shakespeare's sonnet, he suggested that the satisfaction of a lust is temporary; it is "time's fool." Yet the fulfillment of love is permanent, bearing it out "to the edge of doom."[11]

No one ever finds permanent satisfaction without a sense of awe. Yet if they are overwhelmed by this sense of awe to the point of uttering words to live by, then they'll settle not merely for satisfaction but will press on down the road to *fulfillment*. In short, they can hope to one day be *"filled full"* if they can find words to which they feel bound to conform the actions—the service—of their lives. They'll one day be filled full because they'll have found the *form* that God has given for the content of His covenant of love; and it is only form that can be filled—it is only that which can hold the love God pours out that can be filled to overflowing.

Formlessness holds nothing. "Broken cisterns" of broken covenants (Jer. 2:13) allow the love of God to dissipate and become polluted—the influences from all the formless and lapsed surroundings of the broken covenant corrupt love as it seeps from that cracked covenant. Fulfillment requires a form that is sealed.* It is sealed by God's Spirit and the sin-

---

* 2 Tim. 2:21, Ampl.; 2 Cor. 4:7 with Eph. 1:13; Rev. 7:3.

less death of Jesus. Only such a form can hold the reality, the content, of God's love. Form is not the content, but it is necessary in order to, first, hold the content and then to channel it to meet human needs and all those purposes ordained by heaven. So the *fulfillment* of love vanishes apart from the *form* of the relationship, the form designed to hold the love.*

It is central to human society to ask just how any given combination of two or more people is supposed to relate each to the other. What order or form is to hold the whole of that relationship and other relationships together? For most people, marriage and family come to mind, but they are seldom clear about just what form a marriage or family should assume.† Yet few questions prove more crucial, since it is the form that will determine what image the content assumes. So this is a great and pivotal question for any people who would purport to being an expression of the community of Christ. And even within the corporate covenant form of Christ's Body, God will bring us into the individual *form* of our other membership services, our ministries *within* His Body, whether in marriage, family or elsewhere. And all these will relate to other services and ministries only in the order and form

---

* See *An Introduction to the Temple and Its Foundation*.

† See *Saving Marriage, Family and Community*.

of the Body. This is the key to a harmonious and workable community of believers. And the form we accept as that of Christ's Body had best be *entirely* from God, for through every crack where people fall short of what God Himself has given, the life of the community will begin to seep out. At the same time, the world seeps in, until all distinctions are blurred and the community itself dies.

Moreover, without such forms, our individual lives can have no lasting meaning, no enduring significance. When the potter takes the shapeless lump of clay, it, like the earth itself in the beginning, is "without form and void." It lacks all meaning and significance in terms of its relationship to us. Yet as the wheel spins, as hands bear down to press and shape the clay, as the clay takes on form, it suddenly assumes meaning and purpose. In other words, it *becomes* a cup, a vase, a bowl, a pitcher. A lump of inert matter has been *separated* from its natural surroundings and then shaped into a definitive form, which further distinguishes and separates it—even the wall of the pot is a wall of separation.

With believers, whatever form our lives assume as we spin under the press of providential hands serves to separate us for some purpose of God in the sacred pavilion. Like the material clay separated into a form, it now has meaning and purpose. And it is this separation coming from form that gives our lives significance. So the Spirit broods over the deep in our lives (Gen. 1:2, Ampl.). It forms and shapes us into vessels of service for God's purpose, fashioning us into members of His Body "fitly framed together." Then He places the form of our covenant relationship like a ceramic figurine into the kiln of life's inevitable trials—including sorrows, pain, tragedies, persecutions, hardships. These will then fire and harden us in the enduring and durable forms into which His love has shaped our lives as vessels of honor for His *eternal* purpose. If we refuse to stay within the confines of the covenant forms, then we'll crack, or otherwise deteriorate into vessels of dishonor. These are the vessels that have lost their sense of awe and been discarded in the shard-strewn debris of the potter's field. This doesn't mean, of course, that some semblance of what they were intended to be doesn't linger— only that it will never be either fulfilled or fulfilling.

The form of language also shows what I am trying to convey about the importance in God-given, living forms. A language's form is what enables us to communicate, to gain and exchange information and understanding. Words put together without form are literally nonsense. Yet words put together according to the rules of grammar and punctuation, ordered according to the structures of language usage and syntax, are words that form sentences (that is, they are literally more than nonsense). They can communicate sense and meaning.

These rules may have been formulated by people, but they inhere in the given structure of language itself. Thus, *every* language can be translated into any other language because of underlying principles and forms common to them all. The grammar of any given people's language, in other words, only describes what already existed before they formulated anything called "grammar." Nouns and verbs must come together in certain relationships; the phrases and clauses of a sentence must fall into certain precise patterns. Many languages even have special written marks—the commas, periods, question marks and related signals—that further order the sentence and its meaning. They tell us when we must pause or stop. So these, too, indicate form. Every detail, then, of the structure of the sentence stands or falls according to precise rules of form, at least if the sentence would mean much, if anything, to us. Because the sentence has form, it can, then, transmit meaning, even feeling, love, hope, joy, truth, life. So through the sentence's form, vital in*form*ation can pass from one person to another—we can, in short, make *sense* to one another and, in that communicated sense, find a common life, a community life.

In other words, without this communication of information, human relationship and community are impossible. Even those who decry forms must use this most formal of structures to make themselves understood as they denounce form. And just as language must assume a formally structured order to express meaning if the fullest communication would take place and community be formed, so, too, must that community be structured according to a definite form that is transcendently given. In the Biblical view, God is the author of language (Gen. 1:3). God made people articulate (see also Gen. 11:7-9). Moreover, in His enscriptured Word to humankind, He, too, confines Himself within the formal structures of language, which He Himself has appointed, using His own Word to *form* His corporate Body into its ordained order to accomplish His purpose (John 1:14; 1 Cor. 12:1-31). Indeed, when He declared Himself, communicated Himself to the world, He became "*the Word* made flesh" (John 1:14, KJV). So no one can hope to fulfill God's purpose unless they abide within the living forms God has given for human beings. Jesus made explicit the important role words serve in all this when He said that we will "have to give account on the day of judgment for every careless word" we "have spoken" (Matt. 12:36, NIV).

And so, it is through words that we make a promise to God, a promise to confine ourselves within the form that He has ordained for our lives through His Word. We pledge to God, "I stand by the Word that

You have given unto me. I have confessed this Word with my mouth in the midst of Your people, and I will stand by it until it is fulfilled in my life. I will keep *chesed*; I will keep my place in the covenant; I will not break the continuum, the memoriam, of life, the form through which Your love passes and is expressed. Though heaven and earth pass away, Your Word shall endure in my life forever (Matt. 24:35). And I will stand in my place, stand by my word—I will keep the covenant and thereby dwell in the house of the Lord forever" (Ps. 116:12-14, 18-19; 23:6). Thus do we commit ourselves to becoming constituted members of the Body prepared to do God's will, thereby assuming the *form* of the gift and the character that God has created us to manifest.

FULFILLMENT VERSUS SATISFACTION

If love's power is enduring, then the covenant, which defines our responsibility to God, defines the term of duration. As the words of the traditional marriage vow define that term, it is "*unto death*," as Berry has reminded us. That is, it lasts a lifetime. Anything less would make love "time's fool." To live out our most private relationships within the limits, the walls, of an earthly home does not mean we are confined within those walls in *every* aspect of our lives—only in the highest and most sacralized of those relationships. In the rest, like Joseph, we become vines whose fruitfulness reaches over all walls (Gen. 49:22). Even those walls that define the limits of the covenant's circle will see the fruit of the covenant extend beyond the covenant itself.

Such a fruit that reaches over walls, while still being rooted within the walls of covenant, is seen, and even tasted, by those beyond the circle of the covenant. It testifies to them of the *fullness* of God's love and invites them within the circle of love. Fulfillment, as Berry has said, is that which brings to rest all desire.[12] Fulfillment is that which says, "I strive no more—all longing has been filled full." In Biblical terms, we could say, with Jesus, "It is finished"— I have "entered into His rest" (John 19:28-30; Heb. 4:10). So when we achieve fulfillment, desire ceases. The need to return for the momentary satisfactions of our insatiable desires has ended when we reach fulfillment. And so the term of this fulfillment must necessarily be unto death. When it is fulfilled, no more desire remains, no need to return, because all has been fulfilled (Rom. 13:8, 10; Heb. 4:1-3; Rev. 2:10). And so we have entered into His rest (Heb. 4:10).

Satisfaction is, however, the proverbial bag with holes (Hag. 1:6). Unlike satisfaction, with fulfillment, all obligations have been met; all responsibilities and commitments have been completed. We have run the full course. The form of our lives is finished; and so, as Paul said, we are ready to at last be poured out as a libation on the altar of God (2 Tim. 4:6). So ultimate fulfillment can only come with death, only with the termination of the period covered by the covenant promise.

Mere satisfaction comes but must be filled and then refilled again and again because it is lust, it is desire, it is ambition, it is appetite. It is the human soul reaching out to meet its insatiable longings and immortal needs through merely transient human flesh and through the immanent and mortal world. While with fulfillment, the soul breaks through the bonds of mortal flesh to move inexorably through the human spirit toward that *form*, that "fixed order," suspended from the transcendent and eternal down to the world of the immanent and temporal, that form where all at last find rest and cry, "Glory! Glory!"

This form of community and order of relationships is nothing less than the true Jerusalem, the city of peace. This is the living form of the living temple of Messiah and His corporate Body. If no such form given "from above" exists, then all hope for human fulfillment must cease. So fulfillment only comes as the human soul struggles and stretches to reach through the human spirit and join itself to the transcendent God's Spirit, the Spirit that awaits the sacralized entrance of humanity within the Holy of

Holies, within the bride chamber of that temple that God has made—the temple of the corporate life of Messiah in His people. For those who press on to realize the form of this temple in an entire life lived in sacrificial love, in the end, no more desire or works will remain because the journey, the task, will have been completed, *fulfilled*. Only then can they say that they "have *finished* the course" and "*kept* the faith" and that they, with Paul, are now prepared to "be offered" up, "ready to be *poured out* as a drink offering" (2 Tim. 4:6-7, NASB, KJV). Only then can they say, "I have fulfilled my promise and so been filled full by it."

INFINITE PASSION

When a person loses or abandons his desire to fulfill God-given covenantal obligations, he doesn't merely run the risk of enslavement to lust and sin. Rather, such enslavement is as inevitable as night following day. Freud claimed to have discovered that an individual's religious devotion to the absolute demands of a transcendent God was in fact merely a "sublimated" substitute for what Freud saw as instinctive passions and desires, which he called the *libido*. Religious devotion was, to Freud, merely the socially acceptable substitute of what at root were the raw appetites of the human organism always striving for satisfaction. Yet Plato called *libido* "a mad and savage master."[13] So Kierkegaard came closer to the truth than Freud: desires that pull us out of the orbit of God's love not only lead us astray and away from home, but also do so by serving as a secondrate substitute for the passionate devotion due to God.

When you live in a world without the absolutes of good and evil, without a heaven or a hell, without an absolute God before whom you live in awe, you have not only lost the coordinates that would properly situate your position and so give you a destination, a destiny, but you also cannot have what Kierkegaard called an infinite passion,[14] a passion that transcends, and therefore transforms, your own life with all its instincts and physical drives that fragment human life into the pursuit of one dead-end passion after another. So the greatest of all commands is to love the One God with *all* your heart, *all* your soul, *all* your strength (Matt. 22:37-38; Deut. 6:4-5). This, first, commands, then directs, us toward an *infinite* passion that calls for the totality of our lives in order to fulfill all. God created people in His image, making each soul, as E. F. Schumacher noted, a universe in microcosm.[15] So each human being has the potential for this infinite passion, and if this passion does not pour its energies into fulfilling the transcendent God's covenant, with all its givens from above, it will seek substitute cravings and distractions in the momentary satisfaction of blighted passions that can only fragment and break down our lives.

People, of course, have for millennia deified their own animal lusts. So they not only have given themselves over in religious devotion to the worship of such lusts, but they have also fiercely resented anyone exposing the artificiality and cultivated veneer that tries to glorify those lusts as love, or that at least tries to reduce love to nothing more than lust with romantic makeup on, accompanied by mood music. This phony glorification of lust was perhaps first embodied in the pagan goddess worship of Astarte or Ishtar or Venus or, later, the more modernized versions found in the idol worship of rock singer sirens, or the "playmate of the month," or the latest Hollywood starlet or romance novels. When people lose the absolutes of good and evil, of heaven and hell, they lose all clear values of a "black and white" morality; and, as any watercolorist will tell you, if you cannot perceive at least a three-leveled value scale from black to white, then you cannot hope to be a successful colorist, since the success of hue rests on shade. Those therefore who lose the value scale of a black and white, of a dos and don'ts, morality end up living a life equivalent to artistic "mud"—in which all colors lose their vibrancy in a nondescript and indiscriminate moral mix. This mud is anything but a life of technicolor diversity.

An individual created to have an infinite passion cannot long remain satisfied with such a dull and jaded existence. He cannot live with the notion that his life might become nothing but an insipid, passionless and desiccated gruel. So he will seek some transitory passion to fill what is lacking in his life, seeking to inflame himself with mere momentary exuberances, or extremities of entertainments or even the most twisted simple lusts—all because his eternal spirit and soul have died within him. He refuses to give himself over to the infinite passion possible through the confining form of a powerful relationship with God, which always, of course, demands each person's whole being. So instead, he gives himself over, perhaps at first only incrementally, to lapsed passions—obsessive work, covetousness, self-indulgences, lust, impurity, promiscuity, pornography, adultery, sodomy and dozens of other all too finite passions.

Yet such lust can never be infinite. It *is*, however, endless in that it seeks the ever-greater titillation and excitement of further transgression in a feeding frenzy that tries in vain to stop the endless torment of unfulfilled desire. At last, this lust and craving often ends in blood lust. This is what has increasingly become the religion of our modern secular age, what has been called—against the historical background of the "Age of Religion," the "Age of Reason," the "Age of Science"—the "Age of Sexuality," as well as the "Age of Blood." Many, however, would not deny the reasons why the twentieth and twenty-first centuries have been called "The Age of Blood." Enthusiasts for an infinite God have been so roundly hated and ridiculed for so many generations that superiority to enthusiasm has become a necessary stereotype for those worshiping at the altar of their own bodies and minds, never knowing that they themselves have simply become another cliché. But without the enthusiasm for a transcendent God, a person will absolutize some other—*any* other—desire or object of desire; for people were designed to worship, even if they only worship themselves. The fact that anthropologists have not discovered one culture on earth without religion would seem to confirm this.[16] But in choosing to ignore the absolute call of the transcendent God who is greater than the human god, people therefore become addicted to something that almost always becomes far *less* than human. Then their passion turns to the immanence of animal lust, like young terrorists whose religion can only promise them harems of virgins in a heaven that amounts to nothing but an eternal carnality, of wallowing endlessly in what they lusted for on earth. Such people become enslaved to their own fleeting and finite illusions because they have not become consumed with the interests of an infinite God, interests defined by self-giving love instead of self-serving lust. Again, ultimately, *blood* lust will become the obsession of those who have become jaded on every other lust and thus have collapsed into this abysmal state. But even the satisfaction of blood lust remains temporary and must be returned to with ever-greater unrestraint, barbarism, fanaticism and frenzy. This metastasizing condition promises the destruction of humanity itself. Thus, again, "The Age of Blood."

Nor can an infinite passion merely devolve into the negative hatred of evil. Followers of the God of transcendent love cannot hate with an infinite passion. They are commanded to *love* God with *all* their heart and soul, but they are not commanded to hate satan or evil with all their heart. Fulfillment in life only comes by confronting the absolute call of God and then, recognizing that His love is a consuming fire, giving oneself over to the infinite passion of *chesed*, which always seeks to fulfill, to fill full, the responsibilities and obligations of God's consuming covenant. Fulfillment, then, comes only with the *chesed* of a true love, with the faithful meeting of our covenant vows and obligations. Only the love of *chesed* can bring true oneness, can intertwine two lives, two hearts, until they truly knit together in an unbreakable bond. The marriage covenant exemplifies this. Thus it can become analogous to the covenant between a soul and God, and between people as a community and God.

THE PSEUDO-LOVE OF SEDUCTION

Of course, some, even probably most, more than willingly *proclaim* an infinite passion, but always apart from the requirements of an infinite God. This is not, however, the love of *chesed* but rather the pseudo-love of seduction. It offers and seeks only selfish satisfaction in contrast to fulfillment. It is unwilling to lose its life. It does not seek true oneness, the commingling of lives. Rather, it seeks to preserve its own separation from the obligations of love and calls this its "independence." Seduction has no real, compelling power of its own that can serve its goal of seduction, so it must always pilfer from the force of true love in order to counterfeit the claims of the latter's appeal. The seducer shrewdly recognizes the weaknesses and needs (and so, most importantly, the unchecked wants) of the object of his seduction. So he masks himself in a certain superficial claim to satisfy those needs or wants. He uses his God-given gifts to strike certain poses and appearances of being what the object of his seduction longs for, but he lacks the substance to sustain the appearance past the momentary manipulation of the object of his ambitions to serve his own selfish and fleeting ends. During that moment, he basks and glows in the light of the other's illusions about who and what the seducer is. He may even strike the pose of humility in doing so.

Yet momentary satisfaction is the very best he can finally offer. Afterward, the dreams and delusions of the object of the seduction collapse into a heap of disillusionment, pain, fear, bitterness and mistrust. Using the appeal of this offer of momentary satisfaction and the fact that, in an increasingly loveless world, this is all the "love" many will ever know, the seducer seeks to surreptitiously and subtly bind the object of seduction in momentary loyalty unto her- or himself. Yet that loyalty will prove to be a one-sided devotion, a one-sided pouring out of self. It will become a devotion to the seducer of the whole life of the one seduced. The flashy image, the entertainment, the performance, the bribes, the enticements, the promise of new and exciting "freedoms," the thrill of transgression in one-night stands, the empty romanticisms (whether oriented toward body or spirit), may continue. But it is all a manipulation to keep the object of seduction in line for utilization according to the seducer's own selfish ends.

The seducer desires only the superficial aspects

of relationship that allow him to control, that give him power. He refuses to enter into the depths of covenant where he bears responsibility for the consequences, the results, of relationship. Selfishness alone motivates the seducer's view—others serve merely as means to satisfy his desires or lift up his own image of himself in the eyes of those whom he seduces. In the end, however, when the seducer's desire has been temporarily sated, the one who has been seduced will merely feel used, and then he or she will find him- or herself tossed aside as useless.

Appearances and momentary satisfactions can only keep people going for just so long. If true fulfillment never comes, people merely waste away in their decaying emptiness. Then, used up and abused, the one who has been seduced crawls off in cynical despair, convinced that no genuine love exists, that all love is a sham. Seeing all of this abuse and desecration of love, Jesus looked into the future and asked, "When the Son of Man comes, will He find faith on the earth?" (Luke 18:8, NASB). Then He also added, "*Because* iniquity shall abound, the *love* of most shall wax cold" (Matt. 24:12, KJV, NIV).

Form and Fulfillment

This false love of seduction, however, is not confined to the realm of natural love. It now permeates, to almost an absolute degree, religion as well. This is true not only among what many believers would readily concede are false religions and cults but even (or especially) within what many others see as an increasingly apostate Christianity. Rather than finding life through relationship with the Spirit of God, such people find merely a temporary relief from the anxiety and turmoil of their existence in empty theological or intellectual forms, or in a formless sort of pseudo-spiritual emotionalism or in the high-pitched drama of religious hand-to-hand combat where one religion pits itself against another to try to intellectually bring its opponent down while it lifts itself up.

The inadequacy of the first substitute, the empty theological forms, is now more than obvious to most—people, in short, have long since wearied of eating these spiritual menus. Yet how many churches also offer superficial, soulish titillation and cheap spiritual "fast food"—all perhaps even mixed with some truth and experience of God?* All these titil-

---

* This titillation is to be distinguished from true enthusiasm and

lations and fillers, however, only serve to manipulate people's minds, emotions and loyalties. They never offer the reality of fulfillment that can come only through the binding form of covenant and *chesed*, a form that holds and sustains *both* the experience *and* truth of God. Without the reality of a *covenant* community, without the interweaving of lives, of commitments, of obligations—that is, without *chesed*—genuine fulfillment in life remains forever elusive. At best in such circumstances, we only partake of fantasies or temporary satisfactions, and if those satisfactions are never transcended, as already stated, they must finally degenerate into unbelief, cynicism and finally impurity, nihilism, despair and even violence. Apart from the fulfillment that comes only with the "infinite passion" of God, people will descend into the cesspool of every conceivable, corrupt finite passion of human and beast.

Believers, too, will never find fulfillment without binding themselves in covenant to the *form* of a specific place, a time, a situation and a people—in other words, within the *form* of the Body of Christ. This is so because it's only the form that shall be filled with all the fullness of God, the church that *is* His fullness (Eph. 1:23). And this church is made up of people who know what it means to stand by their word.

---

those manifest forms of exuberant worship that flow from an excitement generated only by the authentic presence of God.

The Lord of heaven stood by His Word some two millennia ago; and He still stands by His Word today. His Word was made flesh and dwelt among us, and He bore faithfully the burden to incarnate God's truth in the conduct of His life. He bore this faithfulness out, literally, even to "the edge of doom." So His love was not "time's fool." He bore it out past the ravaging reach of time's stone-cold hand, past death, hell and the grave (Acts 2:23-27; Rev. 1:18). His love emerged triumphant over time as He passed from the temporal into the eternal. He stood by His Word, and on Him a name is written, "Faithful and True." The form that He then fulfilled was the "form of a servant" (Phil. 2:7, KJV). And those who will be His people and bear His name will be a people who stand by their word, fulfilling the form that He filled full—the form of their love service within the larger form of Messiah's corporate Body.

These will not be a people who must be pumped up again and again, a people seeking only the empty satisfactions of spiritual lusts, filling the perforated bag held in the hands of people living in a perforated culture that cannot possibly hold the content of God. Those merely seeking their own interests, like children in a sweet shop, will never know either the agony or the ecstasy of the cross and resurrection. But anyone who determines to know God in this way will soon find their place among a people possessing an "infinite passion," a people that express themselves in lives that stand by words, a people who are faithful to the form, to the covenant of the cross, filling it up and bringing its promise home. They will therefore enter into His rest by entering into an overwhelming and complete victory over the vicissitudes inevitable in any life. They will do so because their infinite passion springs from an infinite longing to live in resonant sympathy with God and His truth. They see that truth as music, a living song sung from the beginning of the world unto the end, the harmonious *form* that expresses the beauty of God's transcendent love and wisdom to the ends of creation.

So it seems that each must come to a place in life where he asks himself this question: "Do I have words to stand by in my life?" Here the meaning of the New Testament Greek word *homologeo* reveals itself—"I confess." "I *believe*," Paul said in quoting the Old Testament King David, "therefore I have *spoken*" (2 Cor. 4:13). And what he had spoken was a word confirmable in acts. It is only such a word of commitment to covenant love that allows our potential for love to attain its fullness, for we know that we will never be perfect until we are in deed and conduct what we can be in God's power. Since we were made to give ourselves to so great a love, and are "dark and vain and comfortless," "idle or mis-employed," till we do, we can never find rest or fulfillment without becoming and living out what God is.[17]

So each must come to a place where he can make the good confession, *homologeo*, literally "speaking the same thing as." Paul wrote: "If you confess [*homologeo*] with your mouth, 'Jesus as Lord,' and believe in your heart that God raised Him from the dead, you shall be saved" (Rom. 10:9, NASB). According to various lexicographers, *homologeo* means also "to covenant," "to assent," "to speak" a "word together with."[18] This confession of "Jesus as Lord" is, then, the pledge of a good conscience in the crucifixion covenant. It is made at baptism.[19] It is not a speaking of "mere words," which Hosea warned against (Hos. 10:4, NASB). No, this is the utterance of *binding* words in a sacralized covenant. So this is not just any covenant but a *sacred* pledge of life in submission to and in covenant with the transcendent God whose love was made immanent in the cross and whom we declare as our Lord. It is solemnly entering a "relationship with sanctions."

Here is the pivotal question: Has such a word with sanctions come forth in my life because I have believed (2 Cor. 4:13)? Is there a word that I can stand by, something that God has called me to: a people, a place, a time, a vocation, a task, a purpose, a vision, a function, an immutable relationship—a *form* of service? Is there, in short, a word that has come forth in my life that has real meaning in the eyes of the God who is the Word made flesh (John 1:14)? Is there an entire and intricate order of relationships that I *know* with certainty to be the Body of Messiah on earth, and therefore that I know and believe with equal certainty transcends in its importance every aspect of my own individual life? And is this a true word or a mere chasing after fantasies in the service of vanity—an attempt to transform some familial, social, ideological, political, ethnic, cultural or other temporal relationship into a substitute for the eternal relationships of the Messianic community, relationships that begin with each soul's supreme relationship with the Head of that numinous Body? Is it, in other words, an attempt to substitute the earthly relationships of a temporal dalliance for the eternal covenant? If they are words we'll stand by with the infinite passion given by God, then they'll be words that, as we keep them, will also keep us even *beyond* the edge of doom. They will be words that "speak the same thing" as the One whose Word "endures forever." It is only with such words that we will have made the "good confession."

Precision and Sincerity

Imprecise words reveal the absence of conviction, and the absence of conviction reveals the absence of faith (Heb. 11:1, NASB). So imprecise words are words already bending and breaking down under the weight of doubt. In short, the one uttering them will never be able to stand by them and therefore won't do so. Generalities, ambiguities and equivocations do not offer the firm footing for those seeking to stand for truth. Only words of precision offer such solid ground. God Himself does not equivocate when He speaks crucial words to a people.* His sovereign freedom is never, as some would have us believe, impinged upon because of His own consistency with His own words. Those who would have us believe so usually show more concern about their own sovereign freedom than God's. As Leo Tolstoy said, theology can become exceedingly complicated and convoluted, as well as vague and ambiguous, especially for those trying to evade God and truth. God, however, has made His Word precise to those who would give themselves to, actually participate in, His voice (John 8:43-47). Although He remains not just a mystery

---

* 1 Cor. 14:8; Num. 23:19; Ps. 18:30; 2 Cor. 1:17-20.

but a *total* mystery to the arrogant and insincere, God makes Himself known, reveals Himself, to the honest because He is sincere and wants to stand by words that His people can understand, believe and trust.

The insincere speak vaguely, ambiguously and equivocally because they fear to speak words that they *must* then stand by, words that can call them into accountability to what they've spoken. G. K. Chesterton said about morality what we have said here about theology: it becomes "terribly complicated—to a man who has lost all his principles."[20] Such people must always speak words that no one can quite pin down, mercurial words that can be interpreted and reinterpreted so as to avoid the necessity of standing by anything clearly spoken. Yet their insincerity is evident to all who walk in the light. Only precise words can be stood by. A coward simply cannot live a moral life.

God has extended His grace to humanity, but He has done so for *His* purpose, a purpose that will manifest itself in specific (and, to some extent, different) ways in each life (1 Pet. 4:10). God desires to speak a word into each of our lives, a word that each one of us can, in turn, "speak the same thing as," a word that we as individuals can "confess," that we can speak back to God and say, "I acknowledge the word that You have spoken to me by speaking it myself; I stand by this word. By Your grace, I will find faith and be faithful. So I speak these words with absolute sincerity; and I also speak them as precisely as possible." Such a word must come to and through the life of anyone who would live for the constancy of love. Yet how many among us can say today that such a word graces their life? If you can do so, then stand up and speak it!

Such words truly spoken would join us to a *specific* place, a *specific* purpose, a *specific* people. Though not every relationship demands total, permanent, immutable commitment, nonetheless some covenants, as elsewhere* shown (marriage is one, but there are certainly others), prove so critical and risk so much to both parties that they do demand such a commitment. Such covenants must be taken seriously enough to impel us to find words that we *know* with certainty *God* is speaking to us, words about which we, in turn, can speak *precisely* and say, "I stand by them; I will bear them out even unto the edge of doom; I commit myself to them till death do us part, because only then will I know that these words shall be fulfilled in my life. Then I shall enter into His rest, because I shall have brought this word to completion, I shall have finished my course. So I'll

---

* See *Leaving the Lonely Labyrinth* (1977, 1988, 2007), *A Garden Enclosed* (1988, 2003) and *Belonging to God* (1977, 1988, 2014), all by Blair Adams (Elm Mott, Tex.: Colloquium Press).

fulfill this commitment and service no matter what it costs, no matter what sacrifice must be made, because only by completing my sacrifice of service, the *form* of my service, can I truly be found in Him, who 'took the form of a servant . . . even unto the death of the cross.'" If we are not so found in Him, then, again, we are simply lost. And only by losing our lives in Him, in the form of His corporate Body, which is the form of a servant, can we find true fulfillment by filling this form full with the oblation of our living sacrifice, the daily "burnt offering" of ourselves in obedience to God.

Yet we know that most in today's culture refuse to bind themselves to any kind of covenant, whether marriage or otherwise. "I want satisfaction *now*," they say. So the quick fix of immediate gratification becomes their myopic goal, not the lasting fulfillment that comes with the *form* of the marriage covenant. Forms such as vows and covenants and commitments are too binding for them. They can't bear any restrictions in their lives that they, at the moment, might find inconvenient. Nothing matters as long as *their* will and wants prevail. Forms such as the marriage covenant limit them to a form and a definition other than the one they might happen to choose for themselves at any "given point in time." So they insist that they must "free" themselves from love in order to "find" themselves, to find, that is, even the bleakest satisfactions of their own self-will.

As powerfully as such an attitude can pull on believers, they must find the grace to unequivocally renounce it, the conviction that this attitude is rooted in a lie. Unless they desire the fullness of God's covenant with all their heart, soul, strength and mind, they will surely lose that covenant, for the focus of many public attacks against the people of God has, throughout the centuries, been hidden in the surreptitious effort to demolish private covenants, whether with land, people or God. As shown elsewhere,* covenant is an essentially private, protective relationship. It shields those who participate in it from external intrusion and destruction at the hands of careless and predatory souls who stand outside the covenant. Within the confines of the covenant's walls, people can feel free to make themselves vulnerable to others. Because of their permanent, binding commitment to open their hearts to one another, the participants in the covenant can allow each other access to the innermost chambers of their spiritual lives. Any total State, then, that seeks to exalt itself beyond the bounds of the legitimate authority set for it by God, no matter what fleece of altruism, compassion, justice and protection it may throw over itself, will inevitably

---

* See *Leaving the Lonely Labyrinth* and *A Garden Enclosed.*

move to tear down the private barriers of covenant, barriers that inherently exclude and limit public or State sovereignty from deifying itself. Of course, there are crimes that no claim to privacy can, or should, protect. But to increasingly make everything private a crime is to really make a private life, a life lived beyond State surveillance and total control, a crime. Private relationships by definition exclude such public intrusion. "Private" comes from the Latin *privatus*, meaning literally "not of the State." *Privatus* in turn derives from *privus*, meaning "separate" or "peculiar."[21] So in addition to the Biblically revealed pattern, even the very etymology of the word *privacy* shows that the church, as God's "peculiar people" (1 Pet. 2:9, KJV), a people called out to "be separate" (2 Cor. 6:17), lies outside the proper domain of the total State. Instead, the church constitutes on earth the ultimate sanctuary of the private against totalitarianism. It is the corporate temple of human conscience consecrated to a transcendent God for His own dwelling place. And it has always raised up a wall against those with designs on creating a total State.

As shown, sacred covenants define the contours of privacy. This sacralized privacy ultimately seeks to infuse a deep oneness in relationships. The example of marriage shows clearly how covenant defines who will have access to a relationship and who must stand outside the bond of commitment. If a State is not totalitarian, then the political contract between a State and its citizens should liberally define the private sphere of its citizens, and it should limit the State to the public sphere. As said elsewhere,* when the political contract more closely corresponds to Biblical values (and all law reflects *some* underlying system of ethical and spiritual values), the private spheres of individual conscience, the family and church, enjoy a corresponding legal immunity from public regulation and intervention. Yet it is also clear that even less explicit, unspoken covenants control other areas of life. This includes simple unspoken agreements between neighbors not to disturb one another at inappropriate times, unspoken agreements between fellow workers on the job as to what topics they can appropriately discuss without conflict and so on and on.

Because of their potential to severely damage lives, however, certain relationships—such as marriage with its lifelong commitment, or a lifelong religious commitment, or the commitment to a State with its compulsory power to enslave its citizens, or even the commitment of people to business transactions of substantial property value—require explicit statements in the form of a vow, a pledge, a constitution, a contract, all of which define the *precise* form of the agreement. They all serve to state the

---

* See *Education Exodus, Volume One* by Blair Adams (Elm Mott, Tex.: Colloquium Press, 1980, 1991, 2011).

extents and limits of the relationship and commitments.

Explicit terms prove necessary, in other words, when risking something valued. This is true whether it be the physical property over which we have stewardship, or the exposure of the inner essence of our being in marriage or the sacred relationships that form the covenantal Body of Christ. By making ourselves vulnerable in such latter relationships, we invest and risk not only a part of our lives but the very core and wholeness of what we are. To seek a contract to cover us in our business dealings while at the same time denigrating the necessity of a covenant for our marriage or spiritual relationships merely reveals who and what we either do or don't value in our lives. People, for instance, who insist on a contract in leasing out their house but deride a covenant in becoming a member of Christ's Body only show that material things are more valuable to them than Christ or His Body.

Many, of course, have grown accustomed to seeing all their choices in life as being merely relativistic with none of these choices requiring any permanence because such people see nothing of any permanent value in their choices or in the lives of others or even in the church or God. Yet even they will somehow still view their *own* lives differently—there *is* permanent value to *that*, they say. There *is* something that needs protecting and covering *there*, something not to be lied to, something not to be betrayed or broken faith with, something not to be exposed to wounds that strike at the core of *their* being and deplete and waste *them* unto death, something not to be squandered and torn apart piecemeal as one stranger after another abandons *them*, carrying away part of *their* very essence with every broken relationship and departure. *That* value is permanent to them. *That* needs a covenant to protect it, after all. Or at least many of them still claim so. They simply fail to afford the same value to others as they would give to themselves.

And the fact is that those who feel no need for this covering to protect these most personal or spiritual relationships can indeed have little respect for themselves; for they have no sense that their life could become a sacred place for God to live. Much less do they see anyone else who stands in relationship with them as having any essential value. They have lost their sense of the sacred across the board and therefore their sense of awe. Perhaps this feeling of worthlessness comes because they have desecrated themselves by prostituting their person, giving access to their most private self outside of God-given limits, selling themselves cheaply in all the ways modern cultures seem to require. Or perhaps the lapsed world has forcibly overwhelmed their lives, leaving them with only the despair and defeat of degradation. In any case, the result remains the same—their private lives have become profaned. They have no sense of anything within themselves that deserves honor, much less awe, and that therefore needs to be protected and guarded. They no longer have respect for anything sacred in their lives or in anyone else's, anything "called God or that is worshiped" (2 Thess. 2:4). To escape this death-dealing mind-set, their whole viewpoint and all its accompanying attitudes and behavior need to die with Christ at the cross. Then they need to be reborn. This is their only hope.

This terribly diseased perspective results in the spiritual malaise so characteristic of the era. If life means nothing, then our investments in it need little or no protection, since we risk so little for so little. Anyone, however, who feels his life has meaning and purpose senses the need to protect the investment, to safeguard it within the confines of covenant. This is one of covenant's great purposes: to grant a value to what some people would otherwise treat as common and profane but to what is, in actual fact, "a worth unknown."[22] If your property that you value stands at risk, then perhaps a legal contract will suffice. But if the innermost mystery of your soul is going to expose itself to another for the purpose of a lifelong commitment of relationship that eventually becomes a family and a community of peoples, then it will seek a covenant such as that of the God-given institution of marriage. Only such a binding covenant allows two people to risk their individual identities in the hopes of becoming one. So to pledge oneself, whether in marriage or to God and to His people, demonstrates that we do value the relationship as "a worth unknown."

The highest example of such a covenant is when a believer turns to God, when he willingly exposes his life to God in the hope that his sins will be covered in Christ (Col. 3:3), buried under the New Covenant of Jesus' blood, thus allowing the new believer to become one with Messiah and His Body. The believer can then look forward to an increasing oneness with God, and the individual's life can find meaning and purpose in Christ. To repeat, such an exposure of the innermost essence of an individual, of one's very being, demands the highest order of protection; for God made the human heart a temple to hold the greatest of all treasures, His Spirit, His love. So Christians, as God's "treasured possession," as long as they remain in the world, must remain *hidden* in the field of the world, covered by God's New Covenant (Mal. 3:17, NIV; Matt. 13:44), by the corner of His robe, by the wings of His sanctuary.*

---

* Ruth 2:12; 3:9; Ps. 17:8; 36:7; 57:1; 61:3-4; 63:7; 91:1-4, 9.

As said, covenant allows a permanence and protection for relationships so that, over time, oneness and harmony might emerge out of dissonance and conflict, or at least out of duality and difference. This integrity in relationships that results from covenant provides a covering for the lives of all those who would seek refuge under the wings of the covenant, under the right arm of heaven's power. In marriage, it takes time for two lives, two worlds, to merge. Conflicts must be resolved. The parties must overcome weaknesses and failings. This is where covenant comes in—it provides the framework over time that holds people together long enough to resolve these differences (or problems or shortcomings) and change their lives, even while love brings them into an ever more perfect union. Of course, many of those differences may still remain intact as diverse complements which constitute a new and greater whole. In any case, covenant protects and shields us from exposure to disinterested parties, until many of the private failings that we desire to overcome have been conquered. Covenant gives the framework for a love that "covers a multitude of sins" (1 Pet. 4:8, Ampl.). All parties must, however, be excluded from such a covenant if they cannot make the sort of commitment, or if they remain unwilling to make the sort of commitment, that would demonstrate the value they hold for such a relationship.

Therefore covenant sanctifies, or, literally, separates, the relationship from harm. By this reciprocal commitment, the covenant forms a sanctuary for sometimes greatly differing worlds to come together, to become one with each other. So the integrity of these covenant relationships provides the sanctuary of communion for all genuine and sincere private relationships: God and people, man and woman, parents and children, as well as believers with all their fellow believers, and even people with creation—these all stand or fall on the integrity of either implicit or explicit covenant agreements.

The permanent commitment within covenant protects those involved. Each can then risk the tremendous vulnerability that all deep relationship requires. When covered by an authentic covenant, exposure in weaknesses and failings doesn't lead to fear of betrayal, rejection or desecration. The commitment expresses the value placed by each on the highest possible image of the other, the emerging image of the God who *is* love, who becomes all in all. So at the same time, covenant declares a sacred obligation to that highest of all images. The abiding love, held and undergirded by the covenant, is all that protects, covers, forgives and heals us as we pass through the "searing experience of self-revelation," experiences of self-revealing that marriage and other such relationships must always at times bring.[23] In this way, covenant forms a sanctuary from fear.

For this reason, a child senses stability and covering within the covenant of family, and so for this reason God ordained the family as the nurturing habitat for child rearing. Within this protective wall the child can work through not only the weaknesses inherent in youthfulness, but he can also work out his character difficulties as well. He can risk, within the secure haven of the family, his first attempts at not only walking, talking, reading, working but also at ethical conduct—honesty, purity, integrity, fidelity—or a multitude of other (to him) monumental tasks and goals. And he can do so without the paralyzing fear of rejection because of failure (as is so common, for instance, in public institutional settings or peer group pressure situations). The only "failure" that demands rejection is the deliberate breaking—through betrayal or lying or open rebellion—of that covenant which holds everything else of value together.

So the marriage covenant gives permanence and stability to the family, which in turn offers security to parents and children alike. Research has shown that this even holds true for a dysfunctional family.[24] Divorce can devastate both parents and children, but even then, the tattered remnant of relationship with even one parent is better than the total sundering of children from both. Every benefit of the doubt must, then, fall to private covenants such as that of the family, especially since no doubt can exist as to the ineptitude of the total State.*

A machine might suffer the loss of only function and utility when disassembled. Even then, someone with skill might restore the parts of the machine to a usable condition or else replace them. Yet with life, none of this holds true. An apple tree chain-sawed to the ground and then stacked next to the wall as cordwood hardly remains an apple tree, or any sort of tree for that matter. This is true even though its constituent parts might still exist in their basically original form, except, of course, for their dissection and dislocation from all the rest and the fact that it will never again bear what gave it its identity—apples. Or take another, more gruesome example: upon entering a room that has a human leg lying on a chair, another in the closet, a torso behind the couch, two arms against the wall and a head over by the stairwell, no one would say that they "just met the nicest person" in that room: the person is no longer there.

Life inheres in the wholeness of the precise *form*—the "fixed order"—of relationships that the parts assume. And so if you destroy the form, the order, you

---

* See *The Crime of Compulsory Education* by Blair Adams and Joel Stein (Elm Mott, Tex.: Colloquium Press, 1980).

destroy the life. Any living form must remain integral if life is to continue. This necessary distinction between the animate and inanimate completely escapes those social engineers (or even some social workers) who desire to apply mechanical principles to society, chopping it up and stacking it against the bureaucratic wall according to designs that make it easier for bureaucrats to manipulate and warm their own souls over in the glory of a false altruism, even while they fill their pocketbooks on the taxpayers' "love" money. Yet since it is covenant that ties us to the *form* of a relationship, covenant provides the integrity, the framework, of the interrelatedness of life. It makes relationship a *living* entity in itself. When you have broken the covenant, you have lost something real and of great worth, for you have lost the very *life* of that relationship.

God has therefore designed and ordered relationships through covenant so that His singular life and love can flow within its contours. Covenants of life—marriage, the family, the religious community—are not covenants of secrecy to hide clandestine intent, but God-ordained covenants of privacy to hold and protect life in the midst of an increasingly dissolute world rife with violence, spiritual malaise, totalitarian control and death. Because of sin's presence in the world, covenant demands exclusivity, preventing infection, adulteration and corruption from penetrating this living relationship. To reject this exclusivity is to willingly embrace a sort of spiritual and moral AIDS, where, through viral attack, the cultural body loses its immune responses, loses its ability to resist and exclude dangerous and death-dealing pathogens.

A correlative purpose of covenant is tied to the fact that the finite nature of human beings means that their reach of genuine relationship is, as Berry has said, necessarily short.[25] So covenant limitations help keep what we most value within the reach of our care and responsibility. They properly order priorities so we can enjoy substantive relationships, rather than merely the illusion of relationship in innumerable liaisons and dalliances, both of which dissipate and render ineffective the reach of our limited capacity for genuinely caring for and loving others. God's order, His covenant, whether for marriage, for family or for the church, makes each order of relationship integral, makes each a unit that has a special life unto itself, like a living cell.

Of course, that life has no lasting meaning apart from the larger context of life in which it is situated. Thus the New Covenant defines the whole order of God's spiritual Body so it can express the very real life that His Word infuses into His people. The church, then, has an integrity and a reality of life that extends beyond any individual member, a life only experienced as love flows *between* its members in that order of relationships designed by God. And only in this plexus of relationships can the true image of Christ emerge on earth—can Jesus continue to come in our human flesh.

Jesus said, "For where two or three come together in My name [that is, under the ordering authority that expresses Jesus' identity on earth], there am I with them" (Matt. 18:20, NIV). He who is life will dwell in this corporate temple of believers, a temple built according to the pattern of His covenant agreement.

Scripture calls the individual, as well as the corporate Body, "God's temple," at least when they conform to the pattern and content of God's covenant. These private chambers of both the corporate and individual temples formed by God's covenant provide the sanctuaries where a fallen, death-bound people can begin to have communion with God's everlasting life. The secure and sacred confines of these covenants provide the sanctuary of privacy where each can know his God. Therefore this is also the place where each can truly begin to know himself and others as well.

Yet it is this very sanctuary that the enemy of all life seeks, like a dread disease, to increasingly invade. These relationships and hearts made holy by the sanctification of covenant constitute the spiritual "most holy place," the place in which substitute and false messiahs have always sought to sit enthroned as god (Matt. 24:15; 2 Thess. 2:4). This literal "invasion of privacy" expropriates into the public realm the sanctified and separated, that is, the private. This makes the relationship a matter of "common" interest. In doing so, it profanes it by destroying the *private* bonds of human relationship. So it desecrates human dignity, leaving only the despair and desolation of isolation and fragmentation—of private relationships repeatedly ripped asunder. The adversary of life always pushes to "exalt himself above everything that is called God or that is worshiped" (2 Thess. 2:4, NIV, NKJV). He does so by tearing down everything sacred, all that is private, in the name of the "public." "Public" then becomes a euphemism for this invader's own authority—his own name is impressed into the very thoughts, consciousness and attitudes of those subjected to his constant informing of their minds and souls, until he is finally incarnated in the corporate man-become-god, the totalitarian mega-State. The corporate "man of lawlessness," the corporate body of a humankind loosed from all restraints, the "public man" now "unfettered" by any sense of the private, has set himself up in the temple of God, the private conscience, displaying himself as god (Dan. 11:36-37; 2 Thess. 2:4). This has left many with only this public viewpoint from which to look at the world, a public viewpoint so thoroughly and purposely poured into their lives and impressed upon their minds, until the private and sacred have no meaning or place at all.

So the enemy of life desires to destroy all privacy. No covenant walls can stand between him and his ultimate goal: "to be like the Most High"—that is, to have total access to, surveillance of and power over all life (Isa. 14:13-14, KJV). Such a global and totalitarian State becomes ubiquitous, with no alternative place of refuge from its pervasive power. The covenant of life, on the other hand, sets apart—sanctifies—relationships, lifting them above the common and profane and into the realm of the transcendently sacred. Isaiah tells us that Yahweh's people will call their "walls Salvation" (Isa. 60:18, NASB), for the walls of their covenants are what "separate" them unto God's life, increasingly excluding from that growing life the death of an ever-descending world. These walls, in short, allow God and His love to dwell in a separated, a private, a holy people. And so these walls of covenant define what's private—that is, literally, what's "separate" and "not of the State." These walls stand impregnable—so long as the believer's loyalty, his faithful commitment to the covenant, does not weaken or waver, even when threatened by torture and death. Thus the great load covenant must bear and the crucial part in human life it must assume.

If we want the vision of the covenant, if we want *chesed* to be the guiding theme of life, then we must take hold of God's specific covenant words for our lives. We must grapple those words to our souls with hoops of steel and then stand by them and conform to them in the words, actions and deeds of our lives. We must, in short, commit ourselves to pouring out the fullness of our lives into the form of this covenant, this covenant created by words to stand by. As said, through this commitment, the covenant form then becomes the one known in our lives, the known form into which we can in faith pour all the unknowns and variables of our lives. And then, when we have done all, we must stand, stand first by His Word and then stand by our word of commitment to His Word of command.*

As pointed out earlier, when we join ourselves to something, we join ourselves to the unknown. So when we join ourselves in marriage, we also join ourselves to the unknown, because we surely do *not* know what lies ahead. If, then, we think we must plan and figure everything out before we make such a move, we shall never join ourselves, we shall never speak words that can be stood by, stood by even into the unknown. In short, life simply will not conform itself to what we think it should be. A life closed to

---

* Isa. 55:11; Matt. 24:35; Ps. 56:12; 116:12-14; 119:89-90; James 5:12; Eph. 6:13-14.

the unknowns that lie ahead cannot be *lived* but only endured. It is not life at all. But the realities of life that we face will never bow down in recognition of our godhood. So we will never be able to preplan everything of life, only then joining ourselves to it, secure in our own plans. We can only see and accept the *form* into which an unknown life is to be poured, so that the form is always there, a form that can shape our lives into one of meaning and purpose. We can, in short, only learn how to hear God and do what He says. We shall never have the whole of life worked out, along with all of the far-reaching "ifs and ands," the unending ramifications of our choices. All we can ever hope to see is the overall form of the covenant that binds us first to the *living God in His people* and then to the immediate circumstance and situation we face; and within that context, a precise word will come to us at vital moments of great singularity. We must then join ourselves to that word and stand by it until it is fulfilled. That is the *only way* that *chesed* has ever come about in anyone's life. That is the *only* way of escape.

In sharing *chesed*, we must give ourselves to the Lord first, sacrificing ourselves to Him (Rom. 12:1-3) by sacralizing our lives into His own self-sacrificing love in His self-sacrificing people (2 Cor. 8:4-5). This means we must then lay down our lives in a living and daily sacrament of love service for our brothers, just as Jesus commanded (John 15:13; 1 John 3:16). So we must speak words of commitment both to God and to our brothers according to the purposes and vision that God has given His Body and then stand by our word and keep the covenant. We must be men and women of *chesed*—of mercy, lovingkindness, faithfulness, loyalty, integrity, truth, steadfast love, covenant keeping. Only God can give us the power to be such people. But He stands waiting to see who will speak words that carry us out into a faith that is motivated by love, keeping *chesed*, making our commitment, our obligation, standing by the words we've spoken.

When is the time to do this?—The time is when you hear His voice: "*Today, if you hear His voice*" (Heb. 3:7, 15). If you hear His voice speaking to you today, then you must drop all and respond to His voice *now*—you must speak words to stand by *now* according to the Word He is speaking to you *now*. If you hear "a voice behind you, saying, 'This is the way; walk in it'" (Isa. 30:20-21, NIV), then by all and every means respond, and do so immediately, before that Voice fades away in its intensity and once again becomes only "business as usual." For this is the voice of the Bridegroom calling and showing you the way to His marriage altar, and He may call only once at your door before He moves on to those who will respond wholeheartedly to His love (Song of Sol. 5:2-6). So if His love knocks at the door of your heart, don't "confer with flesh and blood" but "immediately" respond (Gal. 1:15-16) and speak words to stand by. The arm of heaven is extended to escort you to the altar of an eternal marriage covenant.

Remember, though, that *chesed* is not a word that you stand by in the morning, let fall by the wayside in the afternoon, pick up again to play with in the evening, ignore for a couple of days and kick playfully around a month or so later (Hos. 6:4; John 15:4-5). *Chesed* is the ability to follow through completely and consistently, day in, day out, week after week, year after year. It is the ability to stand by our covenant commitment to serve in *all* circumstances, on *all* occasions. It is "steadfast faithfulness," the mark of highest character, the mark of the faithful God.

Humankind seems intent on rapidly proceeding down an inclined plane of disintegration. The first step in that path is always the breaking of one's covenant with God. The loss of all integrity must soon follow. In the upward path toward redemption, however, the first step is making the *b'rit*. Then the *b'rit* must be kept through *chesed*. God is teaching His people today what it means to be a Hebrew in the sense that defined Abraham's and David's lives—"those who pass over," who overcome. He is raising up—out of a generation more and more enslaved to self—a self-sacrificing people of *chesed*. God is sending forth His Word to inflame a people with an "infinite passion." He is filling them with His presence, and He is saying to them, "Stand by this word—fulfill it in your life." He is looking for those whose lives will speak His love into a world bent on hate and destruction. He seeks those who will declare the reality of His nature, of His *chesed*, not merely today or tomorrow, but also a month from now, a year from now, ten years from now, from this time on, even forevermore. He is seeking those who will also bear it out to the edge of doom, a people who will stand by their word, who will keep the covenant through pain and loss, through suffering and sorrow, a people for whom love will never fail.

Only recognition of the full nature of the *chesed* that God requires of us will enable us to truly enter into the *b'rit* that fully joins us to Him and to one another. Then we are ready to take the great vows of the kingdom. With the taking of such vows (1 Pet. 3:20-21, NIV),* just as when a bride takes on the name of her husband, our identity is absorbed into His life as we become one with Him, taking on His name, immersed into His own very identity (Acts 2:38; 8:16; 10:48; 19:5), the identity both of His self-sacrificing death and of His resurrected life. He is a God of love, of gentleness, of compassion, a faithful God. He has given us His covenant name,

---

* See *Troubled Waters* and *Belonging to God*.

the name of Jesus, of Yahshua, of "Yahweh-Become-Salvation."

When we take this pledge to enter the *b'rit*, to keep *chesed*, it is above all a pledge of faithfulness to abiding relationship with God, a relationship expressed through our submission to His covenant name. We are joining ourselves to God as He has incarnated Himself in a living pattern of relationship, one that is expressed in our collective submission to Him through His name, through His own articulated identity and person.* So when we take on His name, we pledge our unending covenant commitment to Him and to His people. Our covenant loyalty, then, is primarily expressed in our fidelity to specific covenant relationships, first with God, and then with the members of His Body to whom He has joined us in concrete, day-by-day, year-by-year relationships. These relationships, above all, constitute the pattern of covenant love, a pattern that began with our submission to His covenant name. The pattern of covenant relationship constitutes the form to which we pledge ourselves, the form wherein we can find fulfillment by filling up the fullness of our responsibilities unto God and to His people. It is the central part in the great song of Yahweh. God's Word resonates within and through the symphony that is His people.

---

* See *Belonging to God*.

Here is where we shall first begin to stand by a word truly worth standing by for a lifetime as we make the journey of *chesed*.

Many, of course, have sought to counterpose love to form and relationship to pattern.* But when we look at the patterns of relationship to which we commit ourselves in our *b'rit*, in our pledge to keep *chesed*, we shall see clearly that relationships do themselves constitute by their very nature a pattern. Relationships *are both* patterns and forms of interaction between individuals, and they can be patterns and forms filled with love. So our covenant relationships serve to mold and shape us in God's image, paring away what God seeks to free us from, bringing forth the reality of His redeeming love in our lives. It is to and through this pattern and form that we must keep *chesed*.

---

* See *An Introduction to the Temple and Its Foundation* for further discussion of this point.

NOTES

1. Meredith G. Kline, "Law Covenant," *Westminster Theological Journal*, November 1964, p. 3.

2. Kline, "Law Covenant," p. 3.

3. Gary A. Anderson, "A Marriage in Full," *First Things*, May 2008, p. 33 (emphasis in original).

4. Anderson, "A Marriage in Full," pp. 32-33.

5. Anderson, "A Marriage in Full," pp. 32-33.

6. Jon R. Snyder, translator's introduction to *The End of Modernity: Nihilism and Hermeneutics in Postmodern Culture*, by Gianni Vattimo (Baltimore, Md.: Johns Hopkins University Press, 1988), pp. xii-xiii; Alan Ryan, "Foucault's Life and Hard Times," *New York Review of Books*, 8 April 1993, p. 12; Kenneth L. Woodward, "A Philosopher's Death Wish," review of *The Passion of Michel Foucault*, by James Miller, *Newsweek*, 1 February 1993, p. 63; Ben F. Meyer, "Undoing the Self," review of *The Passion of Michel Foucault*, by James E. Miller, *First Things*, December 1993, p. 60; Jerry Z. Muller, "Coming Out Ahead: The Homosexual Moment in the Academy," *First Things*, August/September 1993, p. 20; Alan Pratt, "Nihilism," *Internet Encyclopedia of Philosophy*, http://www.iep.utm.edu/nihilism.htm.

7. Dietrich Bonhoeffer, "A Wedding Sermon from a Prison Cell (May 1943)," in *Letters and Papers from Prison*, by Dietrich Bonhoeffer, ed. Eberhard Bethge, rev. ed. (New York: Macmillan Co., 1967), p. 27.

8. William L. Holladay, *A Concise Hebrew and Aramaic Lexicon of the Old Testament*, based upon the lexical work of Ludwig Koehler and Walter Baumgartner (1971; reprint, Grand Rapids, Mich.: William B. Eerdmans Publishing Co., 1982), p. 111; Mont W. Smith, *What the Bible Says about Covenant* (Joplin, Mo.: College Press Publishing Co., 1981), p. 29.

9. Holladay, *A Concise Hebrew and Aramaic Lexicon of the Old Testament*, p. 111.

10. William Shakespeare, "Sonnet 116," in *The Complete Illustrated Shakespeare*, ed. Howard Staunton (New York: Park Lane, 1979), p. 778.

11. Wendell Berry, *Standing by Words* (San Francisco: North Point Press, 1983), p. 209; Shakespeare, "Sonnet 116," p. 778.

12. Berry, *Standing by Words*, p. 209.

13. Plato, *The Republic of Plato*, trans. Allan Bloom (New York: Basic Books, 1968), p. 5.

14. Søren Kierkegaard, *Kierkegaard's Concluding Unscientific Postscript*, trans. David F. Swenson, ed. Walter Lowrie (Princeton, N.J.: Princeton University Press, 1941), p. 182.

15. E. F. Schumacher, *A Guide for the Perplexed* (New York: Harper and Row Publishers, Harper Colophon Books, 1977), pp. 37, 39-40.

16. William A. Haviland et al., *Cultural Anthropology: The Human Challenge*, 11th ed. (Belmont, Calif.: Thomson Wadsworth, 2005), p. 340.

17. Thomas Traherne, *Centuries of Meditations*, ed. Bertram Dobell (London: Bertram Dobell, 1908), p. 115.

18. James Strong, "Greek Dictionary of the New Testament," in *The New Exhaustive Concordance of the Bible* (Nashville, Tenn.: Thomas Nelson Publishers, 1984), p. 52; W. E. Vine, *An Expository Dictionary of New Testament Words*, in *Vines's Complete Expository Dictionary of the Old and New Testament Words*, ed. W. E. Vine, Merrill F. Unger and William White Jr. (Nashville, Tenn.: Thomas Nelson Publishers, 1985), p. 120.

19. G. H. Parke-Taylor, *Yahweh: The Divine Name in the Bible* (Waterloo, Ontario: Wilfrid Laurier University Press, 1975), p. 101.

20. Peter Kreeft, *Catholic Christianity: A Complete Catechism of Catholic Beliefs* (San Francisco: Ignatius Press, 2001), p. 181.

21. *Webster's New World College Dictionary*, 4th ed., s.v. "private."

22. Shakespeare, "Sonnet 116," p. 777.

23. Mike Mason, *The Mystery of Marriage: As Iron Sharpens Iron* (Sisters, Oreg.: Multnomah, 1985), p. 85.

24. Raymond S. Moore et al., *School Can Wait* (Provo, Utah: Brigham Young University Press, 1979), p. 36.

25. Berry, *Standing by Words*, p. 201.

Made in the USA
Columbia, SC
03 March 2025